Junior NKIERE MAKOLONI

COMPUTER COURSES SECOND YEAR CG

Junior NKIERE MAKOLONI

COMPUTER COURSES SECOND YEAR CG

ScienciaScripts

Imprint
Any brand names and product names mentioned in this book are subject to trademark, brand or patent protection and are trademarks or registered trademarks of their respective holders. The use of brand names, product names, common names, trade names, product descriptions etc. even without a particular marking in this work is in no way to be construed to mean that such names may be regarded as unrestricted in respect of trademark and brand protection legislation and could thus be used by anyone.

Cover image: www.ingimage.com

This book is a translation from the original published under ISBN 978-620-6-72064-5.

Publisher:
Sciencia Scripts
is a trademark of
Dodo Books Indian Ocean Ltd. and OmniScriptum S.R.L publishing group

120 High Road, East Finchley, London, N2 9ED, United Kingdom
Str. Armeneasca 28/1, office 1, Chisinau MD-2012, Republic of Moldova, Europe
Managing Directors: Ieva Konstantinova, Victoria Ursu
info@omniscriptum.com

Printed at: see last page
ISBN: 978-620-8-51707-6

Contents

PREFACE

Computer literacy is a major asset for those wishing to trade, enabling them to work efficiently and take advantage of the many opportunities offered by information and communication technologies. And still in the field of commerce, IT facilitates :

- data analysis: IT tools enable large quantities of data to be processed and analysed rapidly, which can be useful for assessing a company's performance, studying markets and trends, etc. ;
- Communication and collaboration: IT tools such as e-mail, online collaboration tools and professional social networks make it possible to communicate and collaborate with others effectively and remotely;
- On-line sales: IT makes it possible to create and manage e-commerce sites, which can be a major source of revenue for businesses;
- Marketing: IT can be used to set up online marketing campaigns, analyse website visit data and target advertising based on user behaviour;
- Customer Relationship Management: IT tools make it possible to manage customer relations effectively, using databases to store and track customer information, setting up customer relationship management (CRM) systems to track customer interactions, etc.

SUMMARY

This computer course is intended for students in the second year of Humanities, Commercial and Management option according to the direction of school programmes and teaching materials of the Democratic Republic of Congo (DRC), a course taking basic theoretical and practical notions on data recording in a file, how to draw up an invoice, a payslip, a stock sheet in Excel; It also explains how to calculate years using formulas and financial functions, how to present a depreciation sheet, how to type and format text, how to use the internet for certain correspondence and how to protect archives on computer media.

In addition, with all the concepts mentioned above, the student in the second year of the Business and Management humanities will be able tackle all the concepts set out for the following classes without any difficulty whatsoever.

GENERAL OBJECTIVE

By the end of the 2eme Humanites Commerciale et Gestion, the learner will be able to use IT tools to enter and prepare accounting and other documents.

SPECIFIC OBJECTIVES

By the end of this course, any student who has followed it assiduously will be able to :

- Saving data to a file ;
- Preparing invoices in Excel ;
- Draw up the stock sheet in Excel ;
- Preparing payslips in Excel ;
- Calculating annuities using formulas and financial functions ;
- Presenting a depreciation schedule ;
- Entering and formatting text ;
- Use the Internet for certain correspondence;
- Protecting archives on IT media

CHAPTER I

EXCEL

I.1.ACCESS TO EXCEL SOFTWARE

As is often the case, there are several ways of opening an application (in computer jargon, we also say "launching an application"). The most obvious method is to browse the list of programmes installed on your computer.

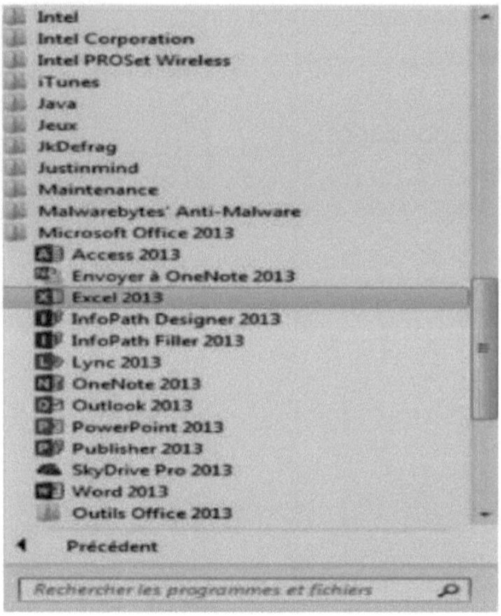

Here's how to get there:

1. Click on the **"start"** button (bottom left of your screen)
2. Click on "**All programmes**> **Microsoft Office 2013**> **Excel 2013**".

A few moments later, the Excel software starts up.

I.2.PRESENTATION OF THE EXCEL INTERFACE

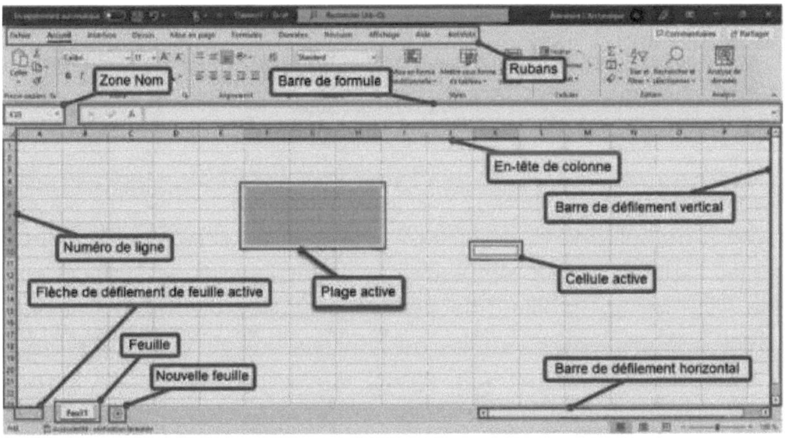

Here are the main sections:

Name zone: Displays the name of the selected cell. It can also be used to name a range of cells with a specific name without spaces or special characters.
Formula bar: Displays formulas and functions for the active cell.
Line header: When we click on the line header (number), we select the entire line.
Active sheet scroll arrow: allows sheets to be scrolled to the right or left; this is very useful for large workbooks containing several sheets.
Sheet: Each sheet has 1,048,576 rows and 16,384 columns.
Add sheet: Adds a sheet to the right of the selected sheet.
Ribbons: There are several ribbons that bring together a wide range of tools.
Active cell: Each cell on a sheet can contain a maximum of 32,767 characters.
Column header: When we click on the header (the letter) of a column, we select all the cells in the column simultaneously.
Vertical scroll bar: The vertical scroll bar is used to scroll the contents of the displayed area down or up when the height of the area is insufficient to display all of its contents.
Active area: This is the area that is greyed out when we select several adjacent cells so that we can manipulate them all together in a single action .
Horizontal scroll bar: The horizontal scroll bar is used to scroll the contents of the displayed area to the right or left when the width of the area is insufficient to display its entire contents.

I.3.ENTERING DATA IN CELLS

You have several options when you want to enter data manually in Excel. You can enter data in one cell, in several cells at once or on several worksheets at once. The data you enter can be numbers, text, dates or times. You can format the data in different ways. You can also adjust a number of parameters to make data entry easier.

NB: If you are unable to enter or modify data in a worksheet, it may be that the worksheet has been protected by you or someone else prevent the data from being modified inadvertently. On a protected sheet, you can select cells to view the data, but you cannot enter information in locked cells. In most cases, you should not remove protection from a worksheet unless you have permission from the person who created it. To unlock the worksheet, click **Remove sheet protection** in the **Modifications** group of the **Revision** tab. If a password has been set to protect the sheet, you must first enter it to unlock it.

I.4.DATA RECORDING

Wherever you save your workbook (on your computer or on the web, for example), all saving operations are performed from the **File** tab.

While the **Save** command (or the Ctrl+S shortcut) you save an existing workbook in its current location, you'll need to use **Save As** to save your workbook for the first time, in a different location, or to create a copy in the same or a different location.

1. Click on **File**> **Save as**.

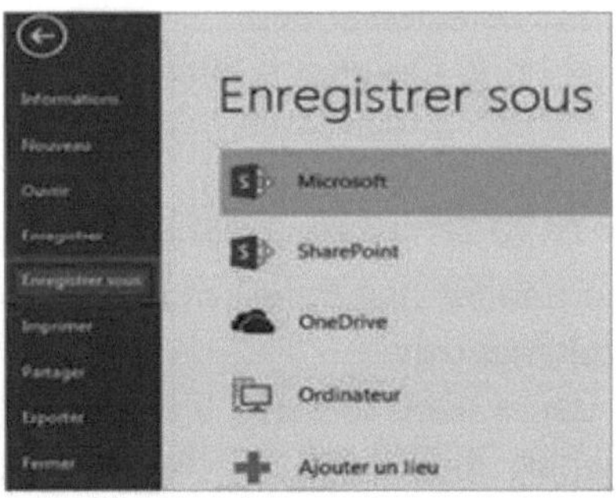

2. Under **Save As**, select the location where you want to save your workbook. For example, to save on your Desktop or in a folder on your computer, click **Computer**.

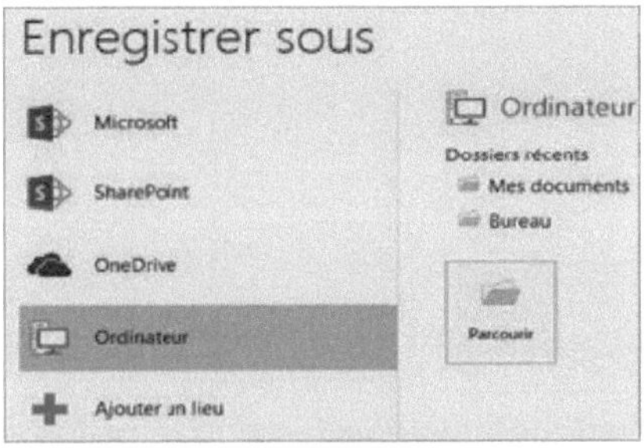

3. Click on **Browse** to find the location you want in your **Documents** folder.

To choose another location on your computer, click on **Desktop**, then choose the exact location where you want to save your workbook.

4. In the **File name** box, type a name for your workbook. Enter a different name if you are creating a copy of an existing workbook.

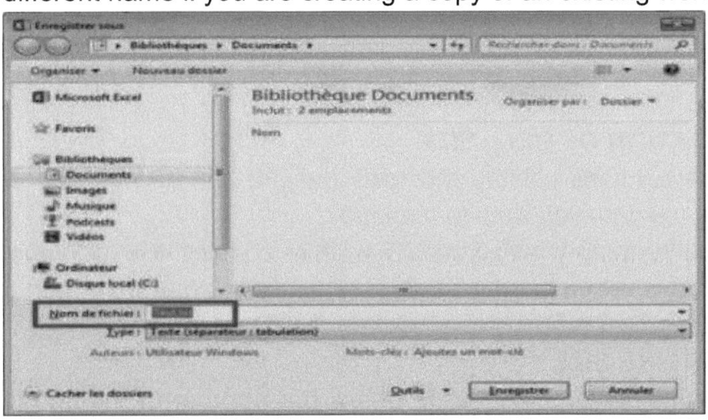

5. To save your workbook in another file format (for example, .xls or .txt), select the desired format from the **Type** list (under the **File name** box).

6. Click on **Save**.

I.5.OPENING AND CLOSING THE EXCEL FILE

To open a file with Excel, **simply double-click on the file**. If your computer has a compatible Excel version, i.e. one more recent than 2007, the file will open automatically.

Just as you can save all the documents open at the same time in Word or Excel, you can also close them all. To do this, hold down the Shift key while clicking on the File menu. Then click on the Close All command.

I.6.CELL SELECTION

To select all the cells in a worksheet, use one of the following methods:

1. Click the **Select all** button.

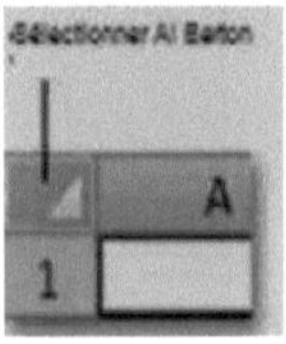

2. Press Ctrl+A.

Note If the worksheet contains data and the active cell is above or to the right of the data, pressing Ctrl+A selects the active area. Press this key combination a second time to select the whole sheet.

I.6.1.SELECTING WITH THE MOUSE

To select a range, select a cell, then by pressing the left mouse button, drag over the other cells.

I.6.2.SELECTION WITH KEYBOARD

You can also use the keyboard combination **Shift+direction keys**. To select non-adjacent cells and cell ranges, hold down the Ctrl key, then select the cells.

1.7. MODIFICATION OF CELL SIZE

The size of the columns (width) and rows (height) can be modified to contain exactly the data you want to manage.

Remember: each spreadsheet sheet is a table of rows and columns**.** Each column starts with a header (A, B, C ...) and each row starts with a row number (1, 2, 3 ...).

1.7.1.CHANGE LINE SIZE

1. Aim the mouse cursor at **the edge below the number of the line** to be widened or narrowed until a **double horizontal line** framed by black arrows appears;
2. Left-click on the double line and hold => the current height of the line is displayed in centimetres;
3. Then **move** the cursor **downwards to widen** the line or **upwards to narrow it**.

NB: You can also change the size of rows and columns using **the "format"** function in the **"Home"** tab. *Click on **Home>** Cell > **Format> Row height***

1.7.2.CHANGING THE SIZE OF COLUMNS

1. Aim the mouse cursor at the **right edge of the column header** to be widened or narrowed until a **double vertical line** framed by black arrows appears;

2. Left-click on the double line and hold => the current width of the column is displayed in centimetres;
3. Then **move** the cursor to the **right to make** the column **wider**, or to **the left to make it narrower**.
Tip: **double left-click** on the double vertical line to **automatically scale the** column **width** to the size of the **longest text** already entered in the column.

I.8.CELL FORMATTING

It is possible to 'format' a cell, i.e. to define the type of data that will be entered in it (a number, a date, a currency, etc.) or to improve its presentation (alignment, italics, colour, etc.).
Let's start with the type of data. The easiest way is to select one of the formats on the toolbar:

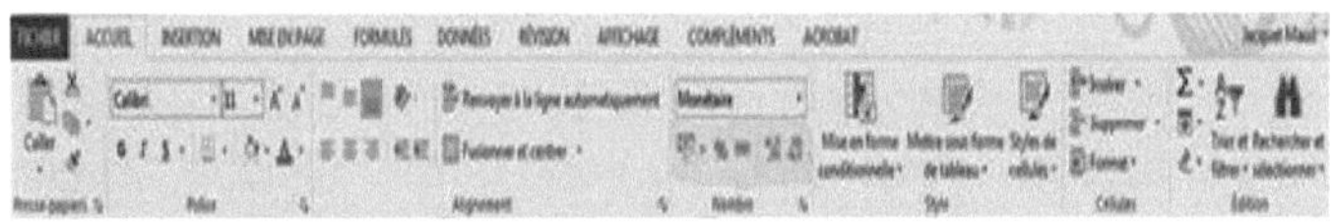

the default currency symbol

Percentage

separating thousands

reduce the number of decimal places

increase the number of decimal places

For example, to indicate that the amount entered is in euros, you need :
1. select the cell
2. click on the currency symbol and select the euro

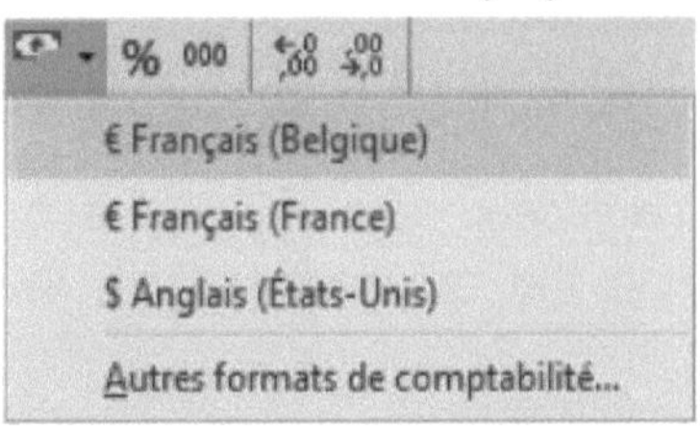

Our amount is now followed by a "€", the symbol for the euro.

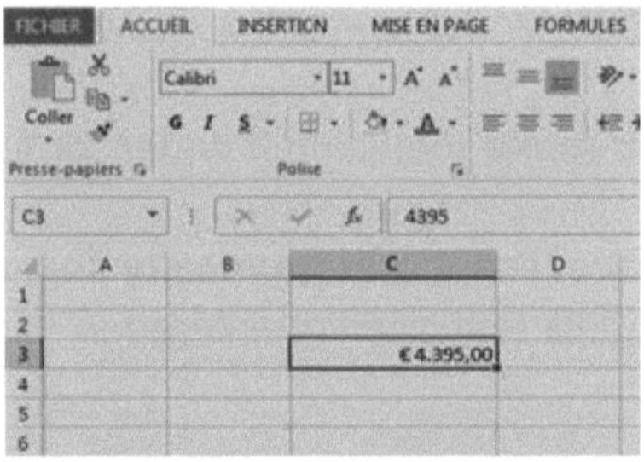

NB: if we want to apply the same formatting to several cells, it is not necessary to repeat the operation for each cell.

We can format a block of cells or even an entire column. To do this, start by selecting the block of cells or the column and proceed as explained above.

I.8.1.FORMATTING

This tool, located in the Home tab, lets quickly apply the same formatting (font size and colour, background colour, etc.) and border style to several cells. For example, you can

Reproduce the layout copies the layout and applies it to other elements of the Excel worksheet.

To do this, select the text or chart whose formatting you want to apply and, in the Home tab, click on **Reproduce Excel formatting**. The cursor will change to a brush. Click the brush on the cell you want to format. Repeat the same operation for each cell. To return to the cursor, press the Esc key on your keyboard.

I.8.2 CHANGING THE NUMBER FORMAT

In the **workbook editor**, you can easily change the number format, i.e. the appearance of a number entered in your worksheet. To do this

1. select a cell, a range of cells with the mouse or the entire worksheet using **the Ctrl+A** key combination,

Note: you can also select several non-adjacent cells or ranges by holding down the **Ctrl** key while selecting the cells/ranges with the mouse.

2. scroll down the **Number format** list G6n6ral located in the **Home** tab the top toolbar or right-click on the selected cells and use **Number Format** option on the context menu. Select the appropriate number format:

- **General** is used to display the data entered as standard numbers in the most compact way, without any additional signs,
- **Number** is used to display numbers with 0-30 digits after the decimal

point or a thousands separator added between each group of three digits before the decimal point,

■ **Scientific** (exponential) is used to express the number in the form d.dddE+ddd or d.dddE-ddd where each d is a digit from 0 to 9,

■ **Accounting** - is used to display currency values with the default currency symbol and two decimal places. To apply a different currency symbol or number of decimal places, follow the instructions below. Unlike the **Currency** format, the **Accounting** format aligns the currency symbols on the left-hand side of the cell, represents zero values as dashes and displays negative values in brackets.

Comptabilité		Devise
- €		0,00 €
- 155,00 €		-155,00 €
10 500,00 €		10 500,00 €

Note: to quickly apply the **Accounting** format to the selected data, you can also click on the **Accounting Style** icon on the **Home** tab of the top toolbar and select the appropriate currency symbol from the following currency symbols: **$** Dollar, € Euro,**£** Pound Sterling, ₽ Rouble,**¥** Yen, **kn** Croatian Kuna.

■ **Monetaire** - is used to display currency values with the default currency symbol and two decimal places. To apply a different currency symbol or number of decimal places, follow the instructions below. Unlike the **Accounting** format, the **Monetary** format places a currency symbol directly before the first digit and displays negative values with a negative sign (-).

■ **Short date** is used to display the date in *DD.MM. YYYY* format,

■ **Date long** is used to display the date in *DD.month* format *in full. YYYY;*

H **Time** - is used to display the hours,

■ **Percentage** is used to display data in percentages with a percentage symbol **%**,

Note: to quickly add a percentage symbol to your data you can also use the **Percentage Style** icon under the **Home** tab on the top toolbar.

■ **Fraction** is used to display numbers as usual fractions rather than decimal numbers.

■ **Text** is used to display numeric values which are treated as plain text with the greatest precision available.

■ **Other formats** - is used to create a **custom number format** or customise number formats already applied by specifying additional parameters (see description below).

- **Customise** is used to create a customised format:
- select a cell, a range of cells or the entire worksheet containing the values to be formatted,
- select the **Custom** option from the **Other formats** menu:
- enter the appropriate codes and check the result in the preview area or choose a template and/or combine them. If you want to create a format based on a template, apply an existing format and modify it as you wish.
- click **OK**.

3. Change the number of decimal places, if necessary:

- use the **Add a decimal** icon

In the **Home** tab of the top toolbar, to display more digits after the decimal point,> use the **Reduce decimals** icon.

Under the **Home** tab in the upper toolbar to display fewer decimal places,

Note: to change the number format, you can also use the keyboard shortcuts.

I.8.3.ALIGNING THE CONTENTS OF A CELL

If you want to realign the text in a cell to improve the visual presentation of your data, here's how to do it:

1. Select the cells containing the text you want to align.
2. In the **Home** tab, choose one of the following alignment options:

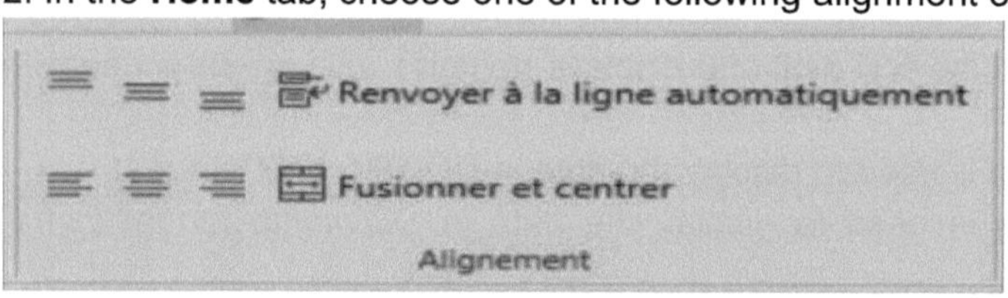

3. To align the text vertically, choose Align at **top**, **align to centre** or **align to bottom**.

4. To align text horizontally, choose **Align text left** **centre** or **Align text right**.

5. When you a long line of text, some of the text may not be visible. To solve this problem without

to change the column width, click on return to **line automatically**.

6. To centre text that spans several columns or rows, click on **merge &**

centre.

Undo alignment changes

- To delete an alignment change immediately after applying it, click **Cancel**.
- To make changes, select the cell or range of cells you want to modify, then click on **Clear**> Clear **Formats**.

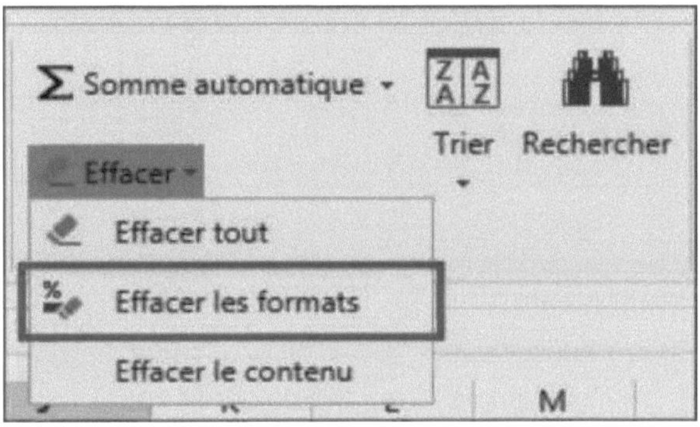

There other ways improving the way text is displayed by applying different fonts or adding a background colour to a cell.

I.8.4.DATA SORTING

The "Sort" function is used to sort a range of cells (made up one or more columns) in alphabetical order, by value, etc.[1]

1. Quick sort

To quickly sort data by the first column, select the range of cells containing the data then click on "AZ" to sort in ascending alphabetical order (from the "Data" tab):

The data is then sorted according to the first column of the

[1] https://www.excel-pratique.com, consulted on 07/12/2023 at 02h37'.

selection :

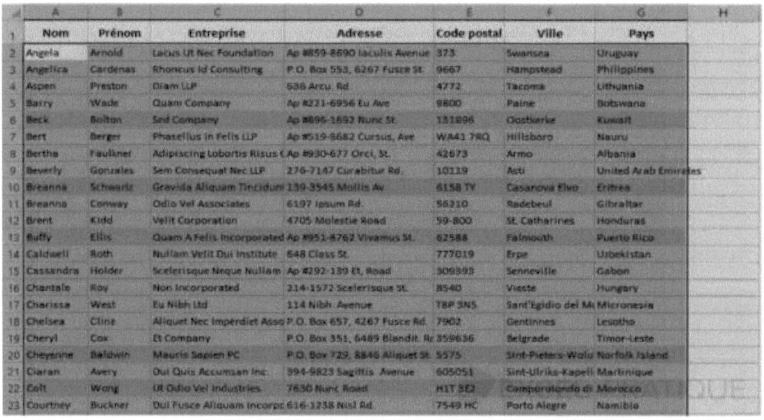

This function sorts the lines of the selection, line by line, without "mixing" the data (you can see this in this example using the coloured lines).

2. Customised sorting

To sort by several columns or by a column which is not necessarily the first, select the range of cells to be sorted (in this case, you can select the whole columns directly) then click on "Sort" in the "Data" tab:

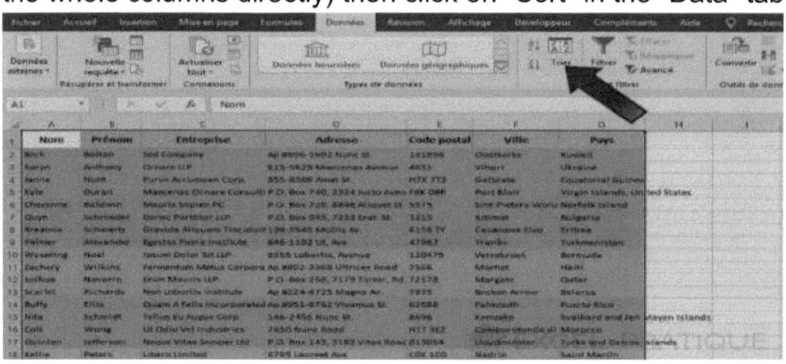

Don't hesitate to select the headings with your data, as these will not be sorted with the other data (as long as the "My data has headings" box remains ticked) and the drop-down list of columns will then display the names of the headings to help you:

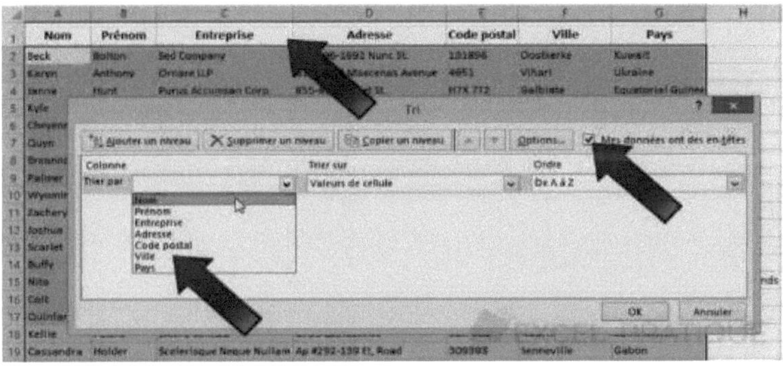

To sort by country, select "Country" from the drop-down list:

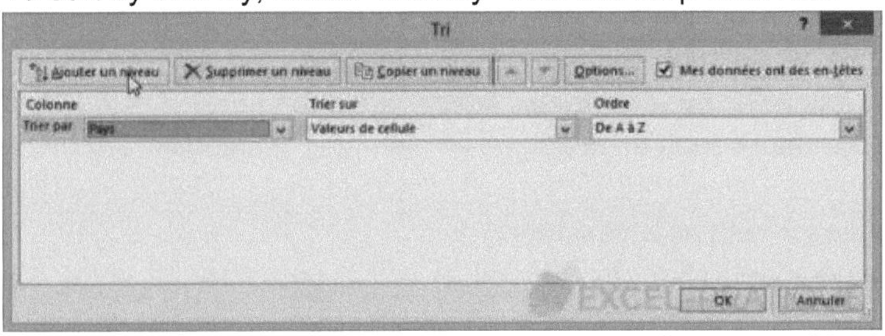

To sort by name (when the country is identical), click on "Add a level" to add sorting by name:

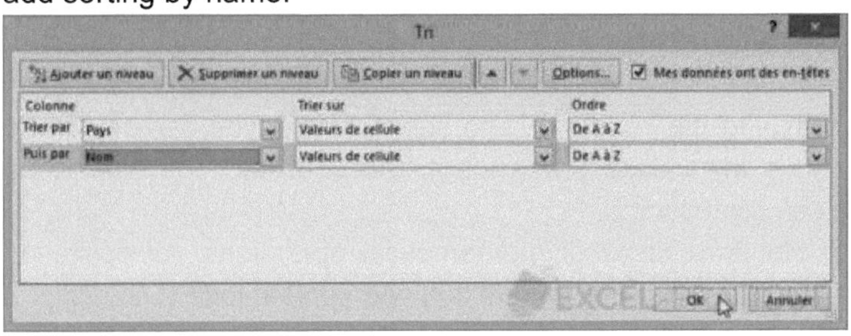

Confirm to sort the data according to the defined parameters:

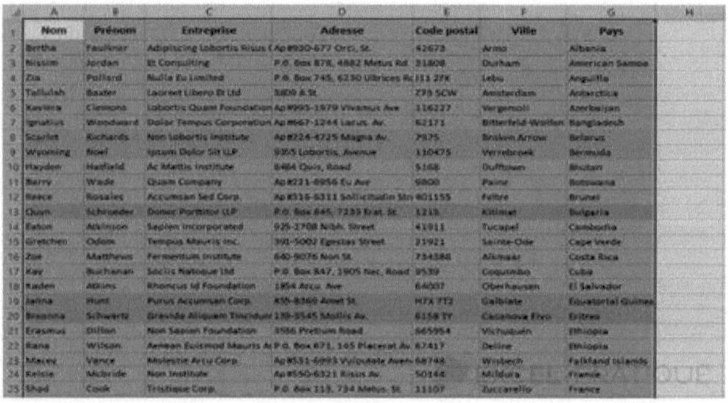

I.8.5.INSERTING A FORMULA

You can create a simple formula to add, subtract, multiply or divide values in your worksheet. Simple formulas always start with an equals sign (**=**), followed by constants which are numerical values and calculation operators such as the signs (**+**), minus (-), asterisk(*) or slash (/).

Let's a simple formula as an example.

1. In the worksheet, click on the cell in which you want to enter the formula.
2. Type **the equals sign** (=), followed by the constants and operators (up to 8 192 characters) you wish to use in the calculation.

In our example**, type =1+1.**

Remarks :

- Instead of typing the constants into your formula, you can select the cells that contain the values you want to use and enter the operations between the cell selections.
- Following standard order of mathematical operations, multiplication and division are performed before addition and subtraction.

3. Press Enter.

Let's look at another variation a simple formula. Type **=5+2*3** in another cell, then **press Enter** or **Return.** Excel multiplies the last two numbers and adds the first number to the result.

I.8.6.NOTION OF RELATIVE REFERENCE

A relative reference is one that will vary when you copy it.

Relative because the cell references are not fixed (A1, B1,) .[2]

[2] https://www.excel-exercice.com, consulted on 07/12/2023 at 2:58 a.m.

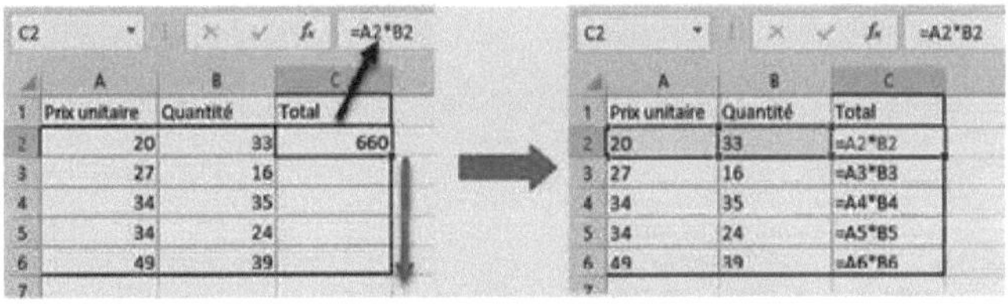

	A	B	C
1	Prix unitaire	Quantité	Total
2	20	33	660
3	27	16	
4	34	35	
5	34	24	
6	49	39	

	A	B	C
1	Prix unitaire	Quantité	Total
2	20	33	=A2*B2
3	27	16	=A3*B3
4	34	35	=A4*B4
5	34	24	=A5*B5
6	49	39	=A6*B6

I.8.7.NOTION OF ABSOLUTE REFERENCE

An absolute reference is one that will not be modified a copy phase. It is also referred to a fixed reference.

A cell is fixed when you put $ on either side of the reference:

=$F$2

$F$2

To position the two $ in the cell referencesimply press **the F4** key on your keyboard.

Example / Mistakes not to be made □□□

To understand the value an absolute reference, we're going to calculate the price (including VAT) of our sales. The VAT rate can be found in cell F1.

Error when copying

The formula for calculating the price of our sales including VAT is as follows: =E5*F1+E5

By copying this formula down we quickly identify that **there is a problem because we have many errors in column F** □????????

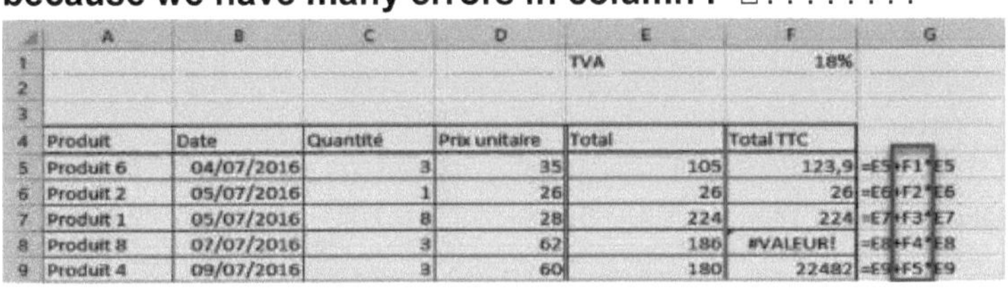

	A	B	C	D	E	F	G
1					TVA	18%	
2							
3							
4	Produit	Date	Quantité	Prix unitaire	Total	Total TTC	
5	Produit 6	04/07/2016	3	35	105	123,9	=E5+F1*E5
6	Produit 2	05/07/2016	1	26	26	26	=E6+F2*E6
7	Produit 1	05/07/2016	8	28	224	224	=E7+F3*E7
8	Produit 8	07/07/2016	3	62	186	#VALEUR!	=E8+F4*E8
9	Produit 4	09/07/2016	3	60	180	22482	=E9+F5*E9

Correcting the error

In this example, it is easy to see that **the VAT reference** shifts when the formula is copied downwards.

Done, to stay with cell F1, we will write our formula as follows:

=E5*$F$1+E5

By copying our formula, we now have **correct calculations because all the formulas use cell F1 ????????**

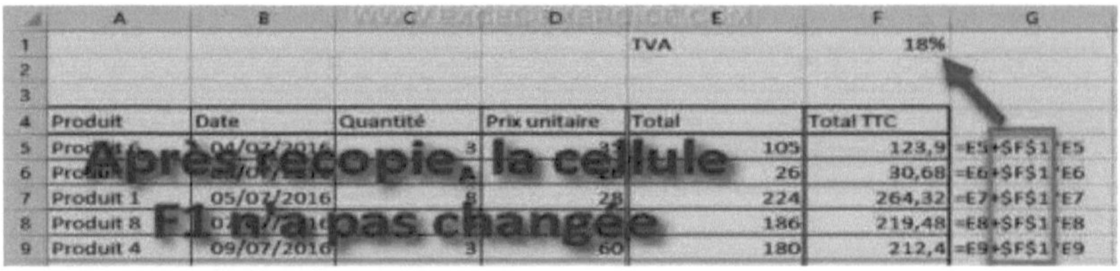

Test to check the formula

Now, if we change the VAT rate to 20%.

. Change the value in F1 to 20%.

Our entire table is updated immediately to take account of the new data, **but the formulas remain the same**. ????

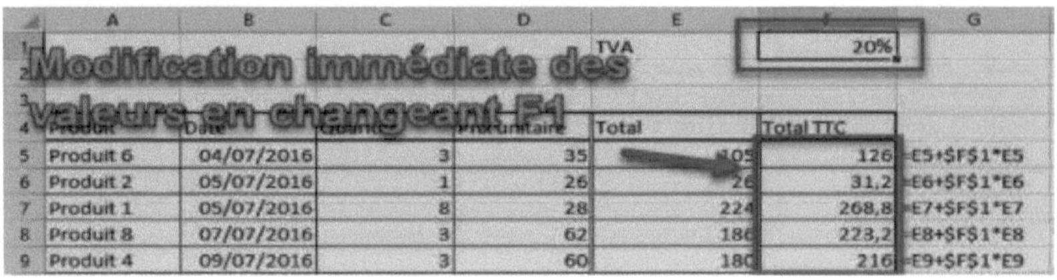

Simplification of the formula

You will notice that we use the total reference (column E) twice in the formula. We can simplify this by using the rules for factoring in mathematics, i.e. =E5*(1+$F$1)

CHAPTER II

PREPARING THE INVOICE IN EXCEL

The invoice is a **commercial, accounting** and **legal document** detailing the nature, quantity and conditions of purchases and sales of goods or services. It is issued by any legal structure (company, association, micro-business, etc).[3]

There are a number of very practical templates available in the software. However, if you want to create a **customised invoice**, you can create your own template.

II.1.DATA ENTRY

The invoice data is entered in the **Transactions** table. For each new invoice, enter a new entry line.

- Enter the **date** of Writing
- **Invoice number**
- The text of the description (items, services, advice, etc.) that will appear on the customer's invoice.
- In the **Debit** account, enter the **customer account** number.
- In the **Credit** account, enter the **counterparty** (Sales, Consulting or other account).
- Enter the **amount**
- If you are subject to VAT, enter the **VAT code** with the applicable VAT percentage.

II.2.USE OF FORMULAS (CALCULATION)

The total for each line is obtained by multiplying the quantity by the unit price.

In the first cell of your "Total" column (H6 in our example), enter the formula **=F6*G6**.

Copy this formula to the last line of the column, in this case to H24. To do this, drag the copy handle downwards.

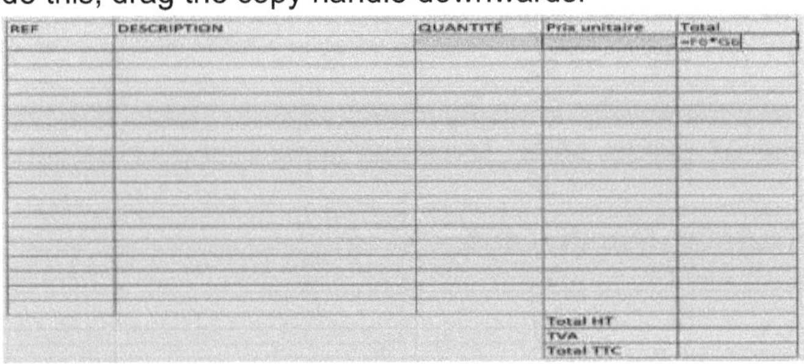

[3] https://intia.fr, consulted on 07/12/2023 at 03h47'

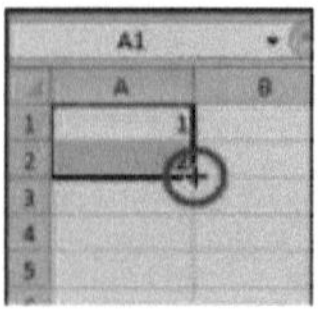

The image above shows you how to copy a formula in an entire column using the copy handle.

- **The total before tax** is the sum of all the cells in the "Total" column. In our case, H6 to H24.

The formula to enter is**= sum(H6:H24).**

- For **VAT**, we need to multiply the total before tax by the VAT percentage defined in your country. In France, the standard rate of VAT is 20% for most sales of goods and services (art. 278 of the general tax code).

The formula to enter is **=H25*0.2**.

- Finally, **the total including VAT** is equal to the total excluding VAT + VAT.

The formula to enter is **=H25+H26**.

Once you've entered all the formulas, here's what your Excel table should look like:

REF	DESCRIPTION	QUANTITÉ	Prix unitaire	Total
				- €
				- €
				- €
				- €
				- €
				- €
				- €
				- €
				- €
				- €
				- €
				- €
				- €
				- €
				- €
				- €
				- €
				- €
				- €
			Total HT	- €
			TVA	- €
			Total TTC	- €

To make it more aesthetically pleasing and easier to read, you can **change the colour of certain cells**. The same applies, of course, to the **font.**

II.3.PRESENTATION OF THE INVOICE

The following information must appear on an invoice:

- Invoice date ;
- Invoice number ;
- The date of the sale or provision of the service ;

- The identity of the seller or service provider ;
- The identity of the buyer or customer ;
- Purchase order number ;
- VAT identification ;
- Description and accounting of products and services rendered;
- Catalogue price ;
- The legally applicable VAT rate;
- Possible price reduction;
- The total amount to be paid exclusive of tax (HT) and inclusive of all taxes (TTC)
- The invoicing address, if different from the company's registered office ;
- Payment information ;
- The existence and duration of the 2-year legal conformity guarantee for certain goods.

II.4.PRINTING THE INVOICE

The following steps show you how to print an invoice; these steps are similar for all your document types.

iOS and Android

1. Touch **Invoices**
2. Open the invoice you wish to print or create a new invoice
3. On overview and management screen, scroll to the **More** section and touch **Print**.
4. Touch **Printer / Choose** then select the printer to use
5. Touch **Print** in the top right-hand corner

Web

1. Click on **Invoices**
2. Select the invoice to print
3. Click on the three horizontal dots ... top right
4. Click on **Print**
5. Select the printer to be used and set the desired print parameters
6. Click on **Print**

Useful information

- The invoice is generated in PDF format for previewing, emailing and printing;
- The default print size is letter size;
- You must be connected to the Internet to obtain the overview, send or print an invoice.

II.5.APPLICATION TO SINGLE INVOICES

1. Launch **Microsoft Excel** on your PC. Once it's open, search for "**invoice"** in the bar at the top of the window to find various templates.

NB: You need an internet connection to carry out the search.

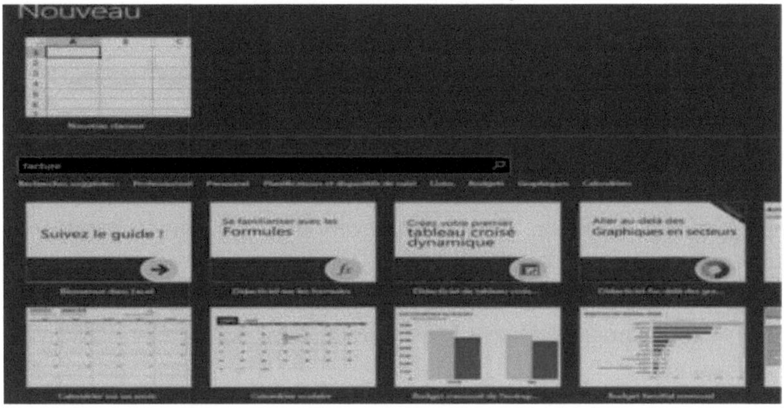

2. Choose an Excel invoice template

Select the model that suits what you're looking for, whether it's for a commercial invoice, a service invoice or an invoice including tax calculations.

Choose a **model that is easy** to understand, so that you can better understand how it works and adjust the elements that are already there. It's also very important to choose a model with a well thought-out design and, if possible, one that reflects **your company'**s colours.

- If you can't find an Excel template that suits your needs, you can always search the internet for a **downloadable invoice template**.

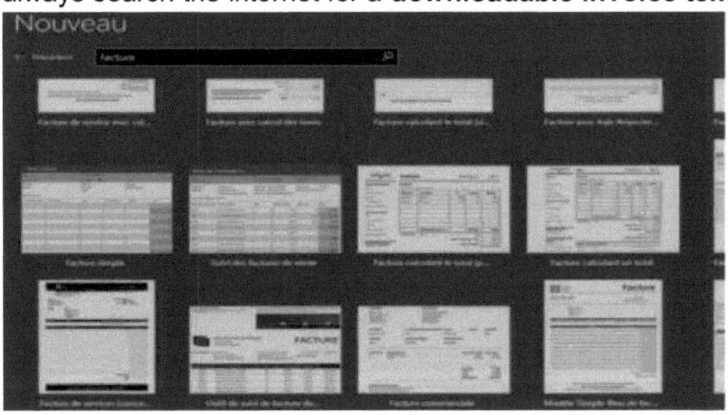

3. Create your invoice

Once you have chosen the model, click on it. A window will display the details of the invoice. Then simply click on the "**Create**button. This will redirect you to an Excel page with the chosen template.

4. Changing the information on the invoice

Now comes the modification and personalisation stage. You'll need to modify the elements entered with your company information. To change the text displayed, double-click on the text, delete and replace with your own text. Here is a list of the **compulsory information** to have on an invoice:

- Name and address of parties
- Date of sale or provision of services
- Quantity and precise name of products or services
- Unit price excluding tax and any discounts granted
- Payment due date and penalties for late payment
- The invoicing address, if different from that of the customer, and the purchase order number if applicable.

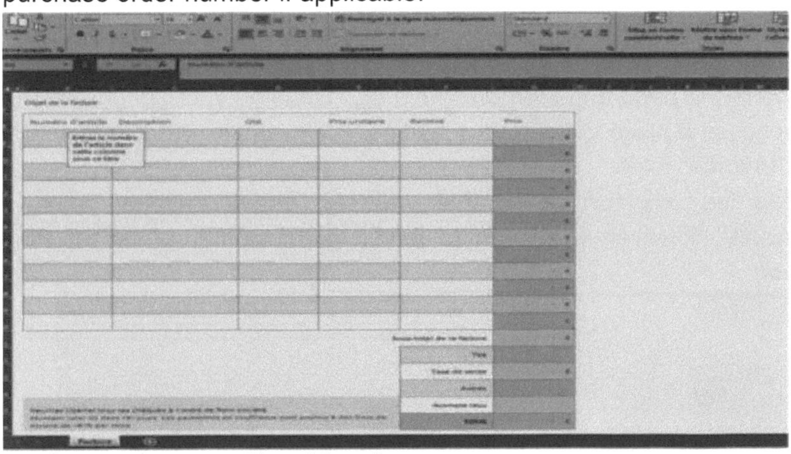

5. Customise your Excel invoice

As far as customisation is concerned, it's up to you to make the changes you want. The invoice should remain clean and easy to understand.

Don't hesitate to **personalise it**, taking inspiration from your brand's graphic charter. To change the colour, go to the "**Layout**" tab, then "**Colours**".

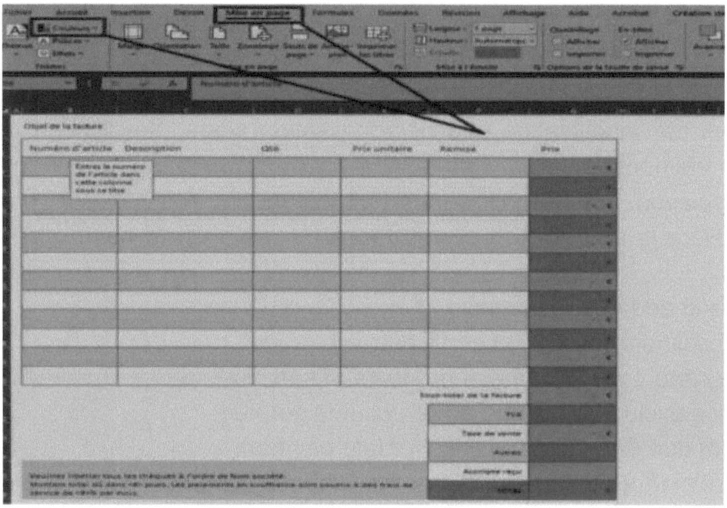

6. Save the invoice

Once you have modified and completed your document, click on "File" at the top of the page and then on "Save as". Rename your document and then choose a place to keep your invoice. For example, you can create a new "**Invoice**" folder.

- Keep the **.xls format** so that you can further changes later, if necessary. However, if you want to send it to a customer, prefer **the PDF format**.

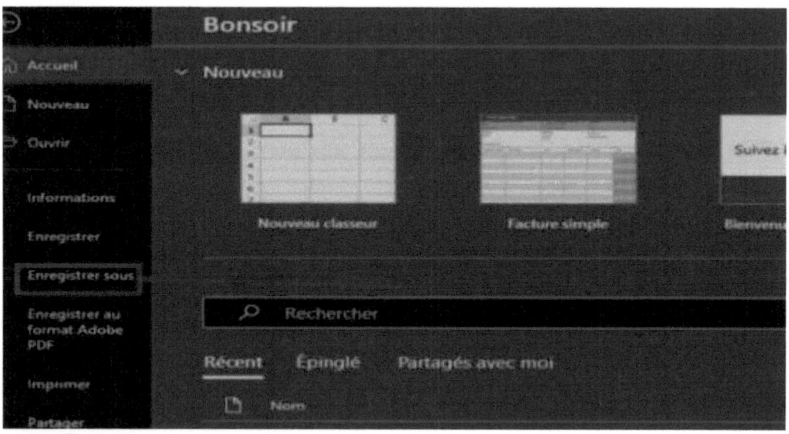

Your Excel invoice is ready.

CHAPTER III

USE OF SI LOGIC FUNCTIONS

The SI function is one of the most popular in Excel. It is **used make logical comparisons between a value and the expected result**. An SI statement can therefore have two results. The first result is applied if the comparison is verified, otherwise the second result is applied.

III.1.APPLICATION OF THE SI FUNCTION ON INVOICES WITH DISCOUNTS (COMMERCIAL AND FINANCIAL)

FACTOR currently prepares its invoices by hand. The company would now like to prepare its invoices in Excel. You have been asked to reproduce the invoice model below in Excel and to automate the calculations as far as possible.

The invoice number, "item code", "description", "quantityand "unit price" columns will be entered, while the other data will be the result of a calculation carried out by Excel. Note that the carriage costs invoiced to customers are 100 Euros if the total of goods is less than 10,000 Euros, 50 Euros if the total of goods is between 10,000 and 50,000 Euros, and free if the total of goods exceeds 50,000 Euros (use the function = SI() to determine the carriage costs). The invoice should look something like this:

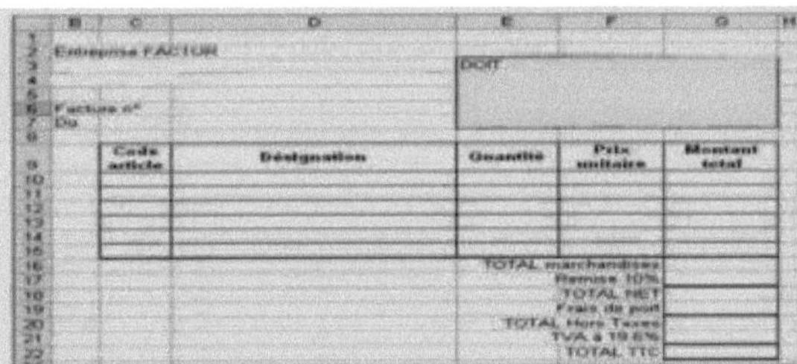

Testez votre facture avec les bons de commande suivants (les TTC à trouver vous sont donnés pour vérification) :

Code article	Désignation	Quantité	Prix unitaire
725	PORTE FENETRE	5	1782,00
532	FENETRE 60 X 120	8	812,00
125	PORTE D'ENTREE	1	2325,00

TTC A TROUVER :19 145.45

Code article	Désignation	Quantité	Prix unitaire
125	PORTE D'ENTREE	2	2325,00

TTC A TROUVER :5 124.86

Code article	Désignation	Quantité	Prix unitaire
725	PORTE FENETRE	35	1782,00
544	FENETRE 80 X 140	50	812,00
125	PORTE D'ENTREE	7	2325,00

TTC A TROUVER : 128 355.32

Then test your table, trying obtain the same results as the following example tables:

Entreprise FACTOR
13 rue de l'Abbaye
06000 NICE

Facture n°
Du

DOIT

Code article	Désignation	Quantité	Prix unitaire	Montant total
725	PORTE FENETRE	35	1782.00	62 370.00
544	FENETRE 80 X 140	50	812.00	40 600.00
125	PORTE D'ENTREE	7	2325.00	16 275.00
				0.00
				0.00
				0.00
			TOTAL marchandises	119 245.00
			Remise 10%	11 924.50
			TOTAL NET	107 320.50
			Frais de port	0.00
			TOTAL Hors Taxes	107 320.50
			TVA à 20%	21 464.10
			TOTAL TTC	128 784.60

Entreprise FACTOR
13 rue de l'Abbaye
06000 NICE

Facture n°
Du

DOIT

Code article	Désignation	Quantité	Prix unitaire	Montant total
725	PORTE FENETRE	5	1782.00	8 910.00
532	FENETRE 60 X 120	8	812.00	6 496.00
125	PORTE D'ENTREE	1	2325.00	2 325.00
				0.00
				0.00
				0.00
			TOTAL marchandises	17 731.00
			Remise 10%	1 773.10
			TOTAL NET	15 957.90
			Frais de port	50.00
			TOTAL Hors Taxes	16 007.90
			TVA à 20%	3 201.58
			TOTAL TTC	19 209.48

Entreprise FACTOR
13 rue de l'Abbaye
06000 NICE

Facture n°
Du

DOIT

Code article	Désignation	Quantité	Prix unitaire	Montant total
125	PORTE D'ENTREE	2	2325.00	4 650.00
				0.00
				0.00
				0.00
				0.00
				0.00
			TOTAL marchandises	4 650.00
			Remise 10%	465.00
			TOTAL NET	4 185.00
			Frais de port	100.00
			TOTAL Hors Taxes	4 285.00
			TVA à 20%	857.00
			TOTAL TTC	5 142.00

CHAPTER IV

PREPARATION OF THE STOCK SHEET IN EXCEL

A stock sheet is a **summary document** and its purpose is help accountants, sales managers and sales staff keep track of stocks and place orders at the right time. In other words, to avoid :

- **Overstocking**: your money is tied up and you risk your products deteriorating.
- **Out-of-stock** situations lead to a loss of sales and are bad for a brand's image. In fact, under-stocking generally results in dissatisfied customers who will not hesitate to go to competitors.

IV .1.DATA ENTRY

Designing the layout of a stock sheet. The stock sheet must provide space for entering the following information:

- Name of item in stock
- Date and quantity ordered
- Date of receipt of article
- Full quantity
- Batch number
- Expiry date
- Date the item was put into circulation
- Number items used
- Stock status (number items still in stock)

Stock records can be stored in an electronic database (Excel or dedicated programme) or in paper form. In the right-hand column, there is a link to a model stock sheet in MS. Word format (for a paper system).

IV.2.INSERTING FORMULAS

The success of Microsoft's Excel software is based on its ability to calculate and display results from data already entered in cells. Excel is great software, provided you know how to use all its features.

In fact, you can calculate anything you want with Excel: just enter the appropriate formula in the cell where you want the result to appear instantly. Formulas can be simple arithmetic formulas or more complex ones, such as conditional and nested formulas. Each Excel formula uses the same basic structure.

1. First of all, you need to go to the cell where you want the result to be displayed.
2. **Enter the "equals" sign first.** The bar in which the formula appears is located above the worksheets, i.e. above the rows and columns of the cells and below the menu.

3. **Now open a parenthesis, if necessary.** It may be necessary to open several brackets. It all depends on the complexity of your formula.
4. **Enter a cell reference.** There are several ways of doing this: enter the cell reference manually. Select one or more cells on the same worksheet or workbook with your mouse. Select one or more cells on another worksheet with your mouse. Select one or more cells on a different workbook with your mouse.
5. **Enter the formula you need.** Whether it's a mathematical formula, a comparison formula, a text formula or a reference formula. For most formulas, you will need to enter an operator. These indicate the type of calculation you want to perform on the elements of a formula.
6. If your formula requires it, repeat the process for each operation within the same formula.
7. Don't forget to close any open parentheses.
8. Once you have entered your formula correctly, press **"Enter".**

Advice

- If you need to use more complex formulas, it can be useful to write the formula down on paper before entering it into Excel. If the formula is too complicated for a single cell, the easiest thing to do, if you're not very experienced, is to break it down. Break it down into several steps, i.e. into several cells, and then fit them together using a simpler formula.
- Microsoft Excel provides you with a valuable aid in the form of ready-made options. These are formulas with "semi-automatic input", i.e. a dynamic list (of functions, arguments or other possibilities). After typing = (equal sign) and the first few letters or a display trigger, Excel displays the dynamic list of functions below the cell. Press "TAB" or double-click on the element in the dynamic list to insert it into your formula. If it is a function, you will then be prompted to enter its components.

You can of course activate and deactivate this function by clicking on the "Microsoft Office" button, on "Excel Options", then on the "Formulas" category. Under "Formula manipulation", tick or untick the "Semi-automatic formula entry" option. This works in Excel 2007 and Excel 2010.

- If you wish to rename worksheets in a workbook containing several sheets, take care not to use spaces. This could be considered an error if the name of the sheet ends up in a formula. Formulas do not allow spaces. Excel does not recognise spaces in sheet names within formula references. You can of course get round this problem by placing an underscore where you want to place a space.

Warnings

Avoid using commas or the dollar sign when typing, as Excel recognises these signs as mathematical functions and will calculate according to their meaning in the programme. In fact, Excel recognises a comma as argument separator and the hyphen or dollar sign as absolute reference indicators.

IV.3.PRESENTATION OF THE STOCK SHEET

A company has many documents that are essential to the smooth running of its business. One these is the **stock sheet**, especially for a company involved in sales and production. What kind of document is it?

What is a stock sheet?

The **stock record** is a document (often kept by the warehouse clerk) used to track the movements of stock items in the warehouse.

It will therefore include permanent information (precise name, location, code, order point, etc.), the date of entries and withdrawals, noted in terms of quantity with references to the documents that justified the movements, and the resulting remaining stock.

What is the purpose of the stock sheet?

To sum up, **the stock record** traces history of goods receipts and goods issues. In doing so, it enables the stock movement to be tracked, and the storekeeper or manager to indicate the quantity of goods available.

Thanks to this **stock management document**, a company can avoid the problems of overstocking or stock shortages. Overstocking prevents the business from operating, as funds are blocked. Stored products can also deteriorate, especially if they are edible.

In addition, **stock records** provide the data needed to calculate the average cost per unit. These data can also be used to make decisions such as continuing to produce or waiting for the stock to decrease.

How to create a stock sheet

The **warehouse** or company **stock record** is therefore of vital importance. For it to be effective, it must be correctly created by the person responsible for keeping stock. Generally speaking, this is not a complex task, but care must be taken to ensure that the table is complete.

One of the easiest ways to create a **stock ledger** is to use Excel. You set up a spreadsheet to insert all the information mentioned above. As a reminder, there should be columns for receipts, issues, dates, name, value, as well as initial and final stock in the table.

Who should use the stock sheet?

In principle, using a **stock tracking sheet** is not complex in itself. However, it should be entrusted to a qualified person, as it requires a great deal of concentration. The employee in question must also be able reproduce the sheet or create one. If they have not created one, they must take the necessary steps to understand and master it in order to facilitate the inventory. The person in charge of stock monitoring and management must be able to explain all the data to his superiors.

As far as the actual use of this document is concerned, the manager just needs to fill in the stock sheet for each movement. is important to avoid waiting so as not to forget any details. All the information must also be entered in the right box to avoid confusion.

Its presentation

1. Product list (names of items in stock)
2. The date.
3. Stock levels at the end of the previous month.
4. Purchases
5. Outflows (sales)
6. Available stock.
7. Average consumption per month over the previous 3 months.
8. Delivery times.

IV.4.APPLICATION TO THE STOCK SHEET

Practice

CHAPTER V

PREPARING THE PAYSLIP IN EXCEL

Definition :

A payslip is a proof of payment that the employer must provide to the employee. This document, drawn up monthly (or according to the pay period), summarises certain amount of information relating to the employee's work and remuneration .[4]

As you know, the payslip contains a range of information and the necessary calculations. But rather than wasting time making these calculations by hand, the Excel software will take care of everything, but don't forget to carry out a thorough check and reread, because if you make a mistake you'll have to take responsibility for it.

Excel is presented as a table made up of a set of groups and labels. You enter your employee's gross salary directly into your model. In other words, their basic salary, including the various allowances and certain supplements such as bonuses.

Depending on the benefits received, they will be subject to social security and social recovery.

So rather than doing the calculation by hand, you will directly automation Execution of a task, in its entirety or in part, by a machine without the need for human intervention. software. You define the applicable rates yourself, and when you enter the first piece of information, the calculation will be carried out automatically, to be displayed in an adjacent cell.

V.1.INDIVIDUAL PAYSLIP

It's important to note that you shouldn't rely on Excel to produce payslips for a company's employees. Only DSN-compliant payroll software can produce payslips for a company's employees.

Creating a payslip in Excel is only useful for specific payroll tasks:

- Learn how to calculate a payslip as part of a payroll manager training course. Even if the educational value is close to zero.
- Check the calculation of certain payroll formulas, for example as part of a payroll audit
- Simulate the cost of an employee as part of a recruitment plan.
- You can also create a payslip on a spreadsheet to go from gross to net pay.

Steps for creating an individual payslip in Excel

Here are the main steps to follow to create a payslip in Excel

[4] https://www.fiche-paie.net, consulted on 12/12/2023 at 02h24'.

- Open Exceland create a new workbook. This requires having

installs Excel on your computer. If necessary, you can purchase the software from the Microsoft website.

- Name the spreadsheet "Individual payslip". So that you can find your way around your work. You can call it "payslip"...
- Create column headings to incorporate the elements that are important for drawing up a payslip. These headings are the contribution bases and the contribution rates. You need to have the elements for the employee share and for the employer share
- Then set the contribution rates. You can also create a database to better integrate new payroll data.
- Use formulas to calculate information such as exempt overtime, absences, social security contributions, the general reduction in contributions, etc.
- Adjust the format of the spreadsheet so that it looks like a payslip. Save the file using a meaningful name and making sure you use the Excel format.

Finally, check that all the information and calculations are correct and comply with the law and any applicable collective agreements.

V.2.SUMMARY PAYSLIP

To recap a payslip, you need :

- Step 1: Enter employer details ;
- Step 2: Enter information about the employee ;
- Step 3: Break down gross remuneration ;
- Step 4: Calculate and enter social security contributions ;
- Step 5: Submitting allowances not subject to social security contributions ;
- Step 6: Mention other deductions ;
- Step 7: Calculate the employee's income tax and net pay.

V.3.USE OF FORMULAS

As you know, the payslip contains a range of information and the necessary calculations. But rather than wasting time making these calculations by hand, Excel will take care of everything.

But don't forget to carry out a thorough check and proofread, because if you make a mistake, you'll have to take responsibility for it.

Excel is presented as a table made up of a set of rules and labels. Directly in your model, you indicate your employee's gross salary. In other words, their basic salary, including the various allowances and certain supplements such as bonuses.

Depending on the benefits received, they will be subject to social security and social recovery.

So instead of doing the calculation by hand, you can use automation to all or part of a task by machine, without the need for human intervention in the software. You define the applicable rates yourself and when you enter the first piece of information, the calculation will be carried out automatically and returned to you in an adjacent cell.

How to use the formulas

The net salary is the salary actually paid to the employee. Employer's contributions relate solely to the employer and are therefore not included in the net salary calculation. On average, net pay represents 80% of of grossgross salary.

The cost of labour represents the gross salary + employer's contributions. The net salary represents approximately 55% of the labour cost. This means that for every €100 paid in personnel costs, only €55 will go to the employee; the rest (employee social security contributions and employer charges) will go to social security bodies to finance social protection.

The essentials

The pay slip proves that the employee has worked for the company. The basic salary is the salary defined in the employment contract.

Basic salary = Number of hours x Hourly rate The gross salary is the basic salary plus additional salary.

Gross salary = Basic salary + Overtime +
Bonus

The basis for calculating social security contributions is generally gross salary. However, for certain contributions, the basis of calculation is limited to the social security ceiling.

Social security contribution = Calculation basis x Rate

The net salary is the salary paid by the employee.

Net salary = Gross salary - Employee social security contributions Labour costs are the total cost of personnel costs for the employer.

Labour costs = Gross salary + Employer's contributions

V.4.SORTING DATA ON THE BASIS OF

1. Select a cell in the **data**.
2. Select Home > **Sort** and filter. Or select **Data**> **Sort**.
3. Select an option: **Sort** A to Z: sorts the selected column in ascending order. **Sort** from Z to A: sorts the selected column in descending order.

V.5.APPLICATION (IN THE EVENT OF A PROBLEM WITH PAYROLL OPERATIONS)

Practice

CHAPTER VI

DEPRECIATION TABLE IN EXCEL

Definition :

An amortisation schedule is a financial tool that details the repayment of a loan or investment over time. It shows the amount of interest and capital repaid for each period, as well as the remaining balance of capital[5].

Thanks to a predefined template, you can check the balance and interest payments on your loans in Excel in the blink of an eye. Simply enter the loan amount, interest rate, loan term and start date into Excel loan calculator.

1. Go to the simplified loan calculator and amortisation table in the Office model library.

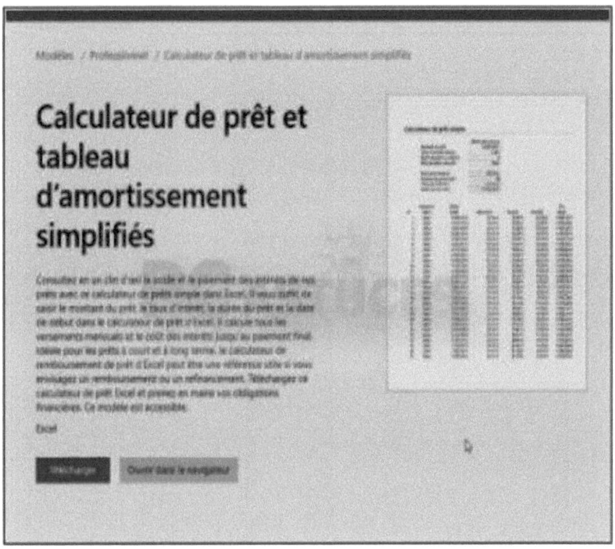

Click on **Download**.

[5] https://www.morpheus-formation.fr, consulted on 12/12/2023 at 03h13'.

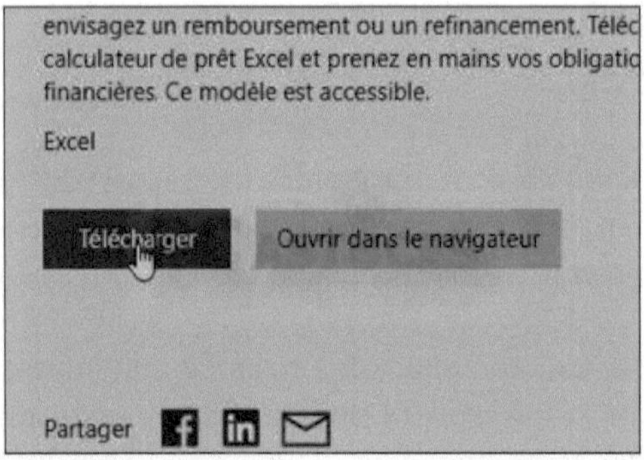

2. Save the model

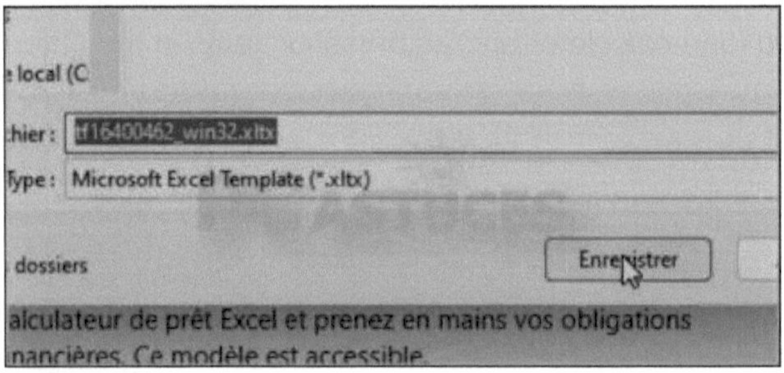

3. Open it.

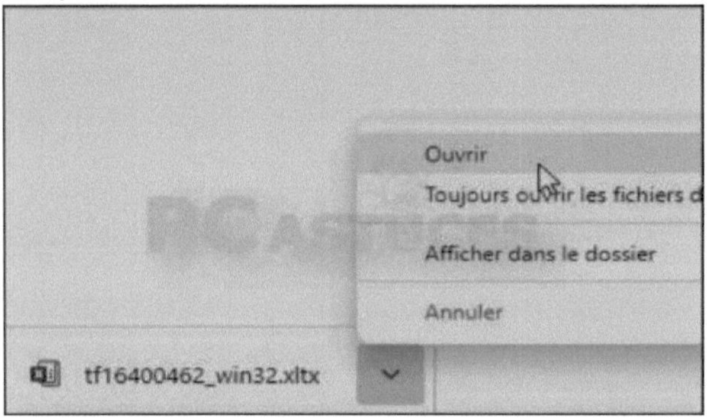

4. You can then customise the table with your values for loan amount, interest rate, loan term and start date.

Calculateur de prêt simple

	Entrez des valeurs
Montant du prêt	10 000,00 €
Taux d'intérêt annuel	2,10%
Durée du prêt en années	5
Date de début du prêt	01/09/2022
Paiement mensuel	175,72 €

5. The amortisation table is automatically updated every month with the remaining balance, interest, capital, etc.

Paiement mensuel	175,72 €
Nombre de paiements	60
Total des intérêts	542,93 €
Coût total du prêt	10 542,93 €

N°	Paiement Date	Début Solde	Paiement	Capital	Intérêts	Fin Solde
1	01/10/2022	10 000,00 €	175,72 €	158,22 €	17,50 €	9 841,78 €
2	01/11/2022	9 841,78 €	175,72 €	158,49 €	17,22 €	9 683,29 €
3	01/12/2022	9 683,29 €	175,72 €	158,77 €	16,95 €	9 524,52 €
4	01/01/2023	9 524,52 €	175,72 €	159,05 €	16,67 €	9 365,48 €
5	01/02/2023	9 365,48 €	175,72 €	159,33 €	16,39 €	9 206,15 €
6	01/03/2023	9 206,15 €	175,72 €	159,60 €	16,11 €	9 046,54 €
7	01/04/2023	9 046,54 €	175,72 €	159,88 €	15,83 €	8 886,66 €
8	01/05/2023	8 886,66 €	175,72 €	160,16 €	15,55 €	8 726,50 €
9	01/06/2023	8 726,50 €	175,72 €	160,44 €	15,27 €	8 566,05 €
10	01/07/2023	8 566,05 €	175,72 €	160,72 €	14,99 €	8 405,33 €
11	01/08/2023	8 405,33 €	175,72 €	161,01 €	14,71 €	8 244,32 €
12	01/09/2023	8 244,32 €	175,72 €	161,29 €	14,43 €	8 083,03 €
13	01/10/2023	8 083,03 €	175,72 €	161,57 €	14,15 €	7 921,46 €
14	01/11/2023	7 921,46 €	175,72 €	161,85 €	13,86 €	7 759,61 €
15	01/12/2023	7 759,61 €	175,72 €	162,14 €	13,58 €	7 597,47 €
16	01/01/2024	7 597,47 €	175,72 €	162,42 €	13,30 €	7 435,06 €
17	01/02/2024	7 435,06 €	175,72 €	162,70 €	13,01 €	7 272,35 €
18	01/03/2024	7 272,35 €	175,72 €	162,99 €	12,73 €	7 109,36 €
19	01/04/2024	7 109,36 €	175,72 €	163,27 €	12,44 €	6 946,09 €
20	01/05/2024	6 946,09 €	175,72 €	163,56 €	12,16 €	6 782,53 €
21	01/06/2024	6 782,53 €	175,72 €	163,85 €	11,87 €	6 618,68 €
22	01/07/2024	6 618,68 €	175,72 €	164,13 €	11,58 €	6 454,55 €
23	01/08/2024	6 454,55 €	175,72 €	164,42 €	11,30 €	6 290,13 €
24	01/09/2024	6 290,13 €	175,72 €	164,71 €	11,01 €	6 125,42 €
25	01/10/2024	6 125,42 €	175,72 €	165,00 €	10,72 €	5 960,43 €
26	01/11/2024	5 960,43 €	175,72 €	165,28 €	10,43 €	5 795,14 €
27	01/12/2024	5 795,14 €	175,72 €	165,57 €	10,14 €	5 629,57 €
28	01/01/2025	5 629,57 €	175,72 €	165,86 €	9,85 €	5 463,70 €
29	01/02/2025	5 463,70 €	175,72 €	166,15 €	9,56 €	5 297,55 €
30	01/03/2025	5 297,55 €	175,72 €	166,44 €	9,27 €	5 131,11 €
31	01/04/2025	5 131,11 €	175,72 €	166,74 €	8,98 €	4 964,37 €
32	01/05/2025	4 964,37 €	175,72 €	167,03 €	8,69 €	4 797,34 €
33	01/06/2025	4 797,34 €	175,72 €	167,32 €	8,40 €	4 630,02 €
34	01/07/2025	4 630,02 €	175,72 €	167,61 €	8,10 €	4 462,41 €
35	01/08/2025	4 462,41 €	175,72 €	167,91 €	7,81 €	4 294,50 €
36	01/09/2025	4 294,50 €	175,72 €	168,20 €	7,52 €	4 126,30 €
37	01/10/2025	4 126,30 €	175,72 €	168,49 €	7,22 €	3 957,81 €
38	01/11/2025	3 957,81 €	175,72 €	168,79 €	6,93 €	3 789,02 €
39	01/12/2025	3 789,02 €	175,72 €	169,08 €	6,63 €	3 619,93 €
40	01/01/2026	3 619,93 €	175,72 €	169,38 €	6,33 €	3 450,55 €

VI.1.DATA ENTRY

How do I enter data in a depreciation table?

Declining balance depreciation table: example for an asset worth €10,000 with a useful life of 5 years

1. first year of **depreciation**: 10,000 x 35% = €3,500. ...
2. second year of **amortisation**: 6,500 x 35% = €2,275. ...

3. third year of **amortisation**: 4,225 x 35% = €1,479 (rounded)
4. etc.

VI.2.CELL FORMATTING

When you type numbers into your spreadsheet, Excel for the Web automatically applies the General number format, but you can change this format to display specific numeric formats such as dates, currencies or even fractions.

For example, if you're working on your quarterly budget, you can use the numeric Currency format to display your numbers as currency values. You can define dates so that they are displayed as a long date such as Saturday 14 December 2013 or a short date of 14/12/13. Here's how to do it:

1. Select the cell or cells you want to format.

2. Right-click anywhere in the highlighted cell range. From the shortcut menu, select the format of your choice, then **OK.**

Note: By applying a numeric format, you only change the way the number is displayed and not the actual cell values that Excel for the Web uses for calculations.

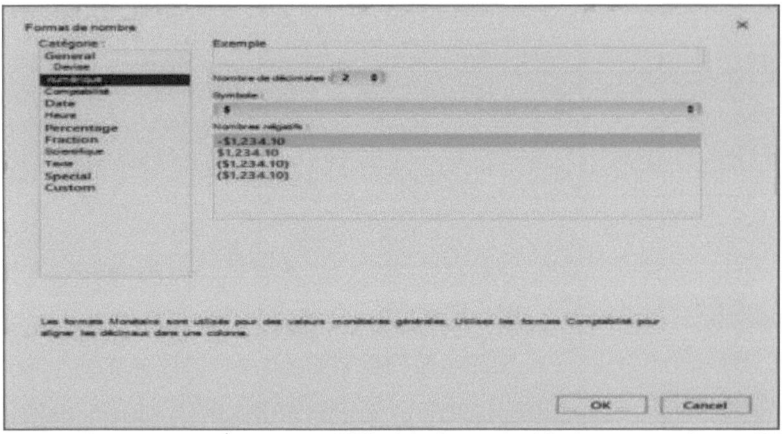

Note: If some numbers are ###, this is probably because the cell is not wide enough. To adjust the numbers automatically, double-click on the right-hand border of the column header. You can also use the pointer to drag the border or right-click on the header and use the shortcut menu that appears.

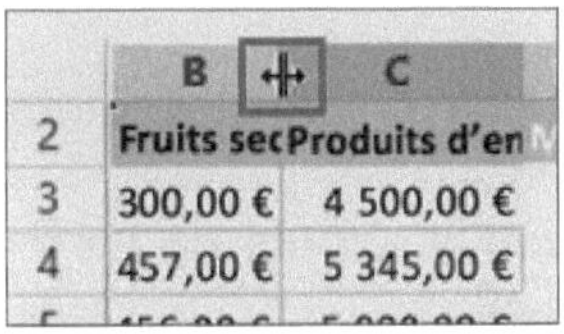

	B	C
2	Fruits sec	Produits d'en
3	300,00 €	4 500,00 €
4	457,00 €	5 345,00 €

VI.3.IMPROVED PRESENTATION OF THE AMORTISATION SCHEDULE (HEADER, FOOTER, ETC.)

Here's **an example of how to calculate the amortisation table** for a €150,000 mortgage borrowed over 20 years, i.e. 240 instalments, with an APR of 1.10%.

Month	Monthly	Interests	Amortised capital	Rest of the
Month 1	697 $	138 $	559 $	149 441 $
Month 2	697 $	138 $	559 $	148 881 $
Month 3	697 $	138 $	559 $	148 321 $
Month 4	697 $	138 $	561 $	147 761 $
Month 5	697 $	138 $	561 $	147 200 $
Month 6	697 $	138 $	562 $	146 638 $
Month 240 Year 20	697 $	1$	696 $	0$

In this example of an amortisation table, the monthly payment is €697 for a loan cost of €17,173. This estimate is based on the information entered in this calculation tool. The table below shows the amortised capital, the interest repaid by the borrower and the amount outstanding. This result is not an offer of credit, but an example of a repayment schedule.

VI .4.CALCULATION OF ANNUITIES

Definition :

In accounting, the term annuity refers to a sum money paid annually by a borrower to repay a debt. In other words, annuities are a series of payments made to repay a loan .[6]

The formula for calculating linear depreciation is relatively simple: **depreciable base x linear depreciation = depreciation year**. The depreciable base corresponds to the gross value of the asset (purchase value excluding VAT and ancillary costs).

---

6 https://www.sage.com, consulted on 13/12/2023 at 03h48'.

CHAPTER VII

REMINDER

VII .1.STARTING UP THE COMPUTER

It may sound simple, but when you're sitting in front of a computer for the first time, you can sometimes wonder how to switch it on...
As with many other appliances (televisions, hi-fi systems, monitors, etc.), you need to press the "**On-Off**" button Φ

- On a **desktop computer**, this button is usually on the front of the tower. In some cases, a small indicator light indicates that the device is undervoltage.

- On a **laptop**, this button is usually on the left or right above the keyboard.

VII.2.LAUNCHING MS WORD

There are different ways of launching MS Word.

A. WITH THE START MENU (With Windows 10)

The most conventional way of launching Word is from the Start menu. Click on **Start**> **All programs**> **Microsoft Office**> **Microsoft Word** (see figure below)

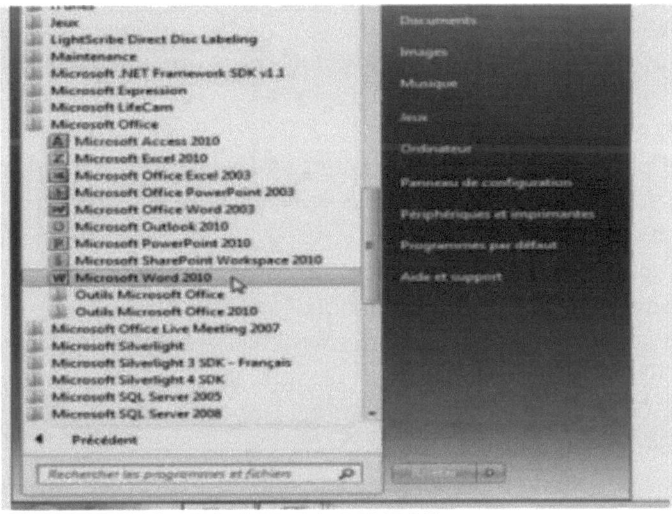

B. STARTING FROM THE DESKTOP

If there is a Word icon on the Windows desktop, you can double-click it to open the application (see figure below).

V II.3.DATA ENTRY (PER KILOMETRE)

Typing by the kilometre (also known as "typing by the kilometre") is a working method which involves **writing your text without worrying about formatting** (at least not too much). Understand that when you're writing a document in Word, you're going to type your text concentrating mainly on the content, on the message you want to get across to your readership .[7]

This applies equally to a covering letter, a memoir, an administrative document, a complaint, a job application, a recipe collection, a book... and any other type of document.

In this way, and because you're only doing one thing at a time (i.e. thinking about your text and not how it should be displayed), **you gain in quality, efficiency and productivity.**

V II.4.ENTRY (WITHOUT KILOMETRE STRIKE)

Definition: Text input consists of transcribing and recording on a medium coming from another source.

[7] https://www.memoclic.com, consulted on 13/12/2023 at 04h00'

Text input glossary

Entering text involves a number of specific techniques and vocabulary, which you can find below.

What is the left mouse button used for?

The left mouse button is used to click. Often performed with the index finger of the right hand, it is used to make a selection while typing.

What is the text entry zone?

An input zone represents the area in which you can enter characters.

What word processing software is available?

As well as Microsoft Word, which is the most widely used, there are other programs for processing text. There's Google Docs, Zoho Writer, Dropbox Paper, OpenOffice, WPS Office Writer, LibreOffice Writer...

What is extended pressure?

The mouse must be held down to select text during an input operation.

How do I select text with a mouse?

The cursor must first be positioned in front of the first word. Then hold the mouse down with a left click while dragging along the text to be selected.

How do I create italics?

Select the text you want to italicise and press Ctrl+I at the same time.

What are characters?

In input mode, characters include letters, numbers, spaces and punctuation.

How do I make a line break in Word?

Simply press the Enter key on the right-hand side of the keyboard to make a line break in Word.

V II.5.SELECTING A TEXT

In Word, you can select all the text in a document (Ctrl+A), or select text or specific elements of a table using the mouse or keyboard. You can also select text or elements located at different points. For example, you can select a paragraph on one page and a sentence on another.

Select all text

1. Click anywhere in the document.
2. Press Ctrl+A on your keyboard to select all the text in the document.

Selecting a specific text

You can also select a word, a line of text or one or more specific paragraphs.

1. Place your cursor in front of the first letter of the word, sentence or paragraphs you want to select.

2. Click and hold the mouse button while you drag the cursor to select the text of your choice.

Other ways of selecting text

- To select a single word, quickly double-click on it.
- To select a line of text, place your cursor at the beginning of the line, then press Shift+Arrow down.
- To select a paragraph, place your cursor at the beginning of the paragraph, then press Ctrl+Shift+Down arrow.

VII.5.1.MODIFYING STYLE, SIZE, FONT, COLOUR

VII. 5.1.1. MODIFYING THE STYLE

You can modify a style directly in the Styles gallery, without using the text in your document.

1. In the **Home** tab, right-click on a style in the Styles gallery, then click **Edit**.

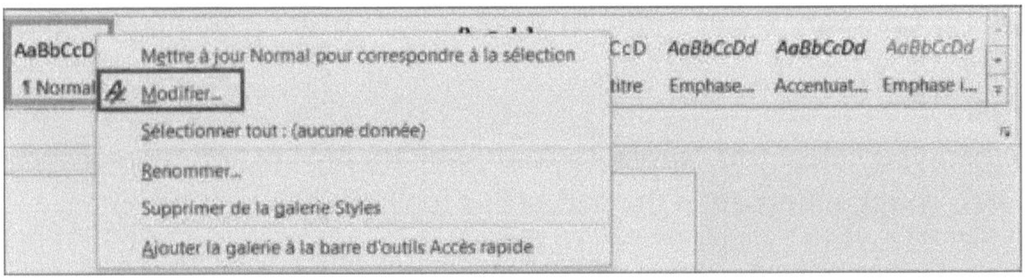

2. In the **Formatting** section, make the desired formatting changes (for example, font style, size or colour, alignment, line spacing or indentation).

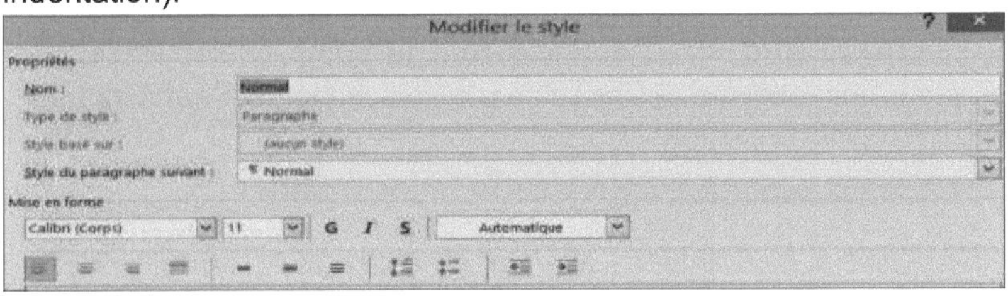

3. Indicate whether the style change should apply to the current document or to all future documents.

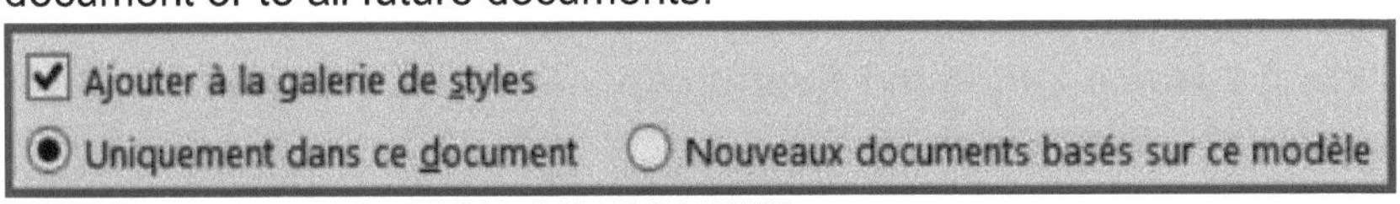

VII.5.1.2. MODIFICATION OF THE SIZE

To change the font size of text selected in Excel, PowerPoint or Word :

1. Select the text or cells whose text you want to change. To select all

the text in a Word document, press Ctrl +A.

2. In the **Home** tab , click on the font size in the **Font size** area .

You can also type any size you like, within the following limits:

- Excel: between 1 and 409, between 1 and 409, in multiples of .5 (for example, 10.5 or 105.5)
- PowerPoint: between 1 and 3600, in multiples of .1 (for example, 10.3 or 105.7)
- Word: between 1 and 1638, in multiples of .5 (for example, 10.5 or 105.5)

Advice :

- When you select text, a mini-toolbar appears next to your cursor. You can also change the size of the text in this toolbar

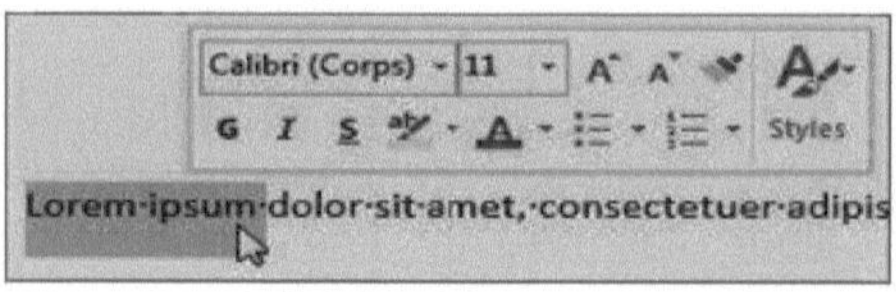

- You can also click on the **Increase** font **size** or **Decrease font size** icons (**Increase font** and **Decrease font** in some earlier versions of Office programs) until the desired size is displayed in the Font **size** box.

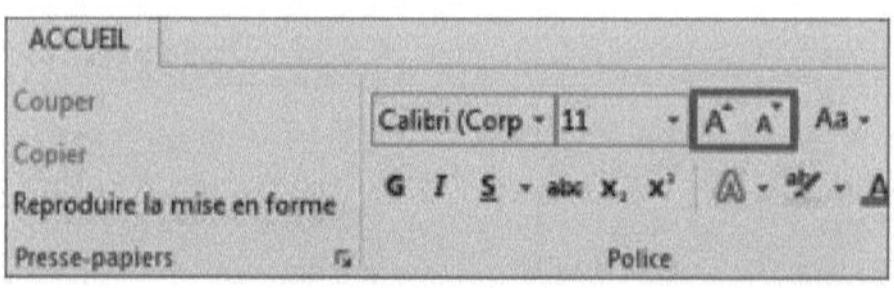

VII.5.1.3. CHANGING THE COLOUR OF A TEXT

You can change the colour of the text in your Word document.

1. Select the text you wish to modify.

2. On the **Home** tab, in the **Font** group, select the arrow next to **Font colour**, then select a colour.

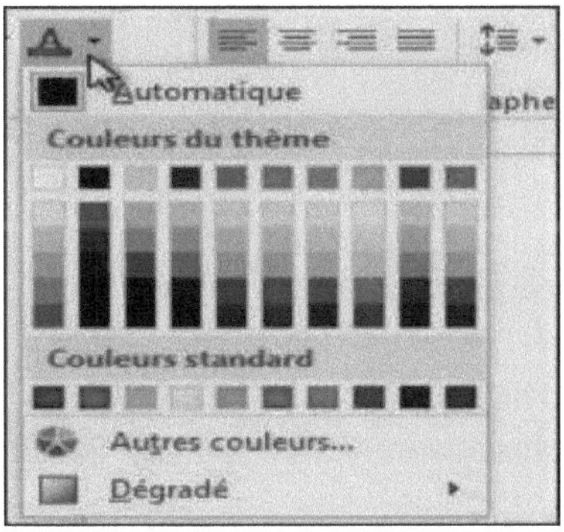

You can also use the formatting options in the mini-toolbar to quickly format text. The mini-toolbar is automatically displayed when you select text.

Advice :

▪ If you don't see the colour you want, select **Other colours**, then a colour from the **Standard** tab, or combine your own colour from the **Custom** tab.

▪ To change the colour, transparency and shadow of the text, select **Degrade**. The Degrade tool is not available in Word 2007.

V II.5.2 UNDERLINING TEXT

To underline text, simply tap on the text you want to be underlined. Click and drag on the text you want to underline to highlight your selection. Press the "CTRL" key and the "U" key on your keyboard at the same time. To stop underlining, press "CTRL" and "U" again. To underline using the Microsoft Word menus, click and drag under the text you want to be underlined to highlight your selection. Click on the "Home" tab on the left-hand side of the Ribbon. Click on the "U or S" button on the left-hand side of the Ribbon under the "Font" category.

V II.5.3.ALIGNMENT OF PARAGRAPHS

Text alignment is a paragraph formatting attribute that determines the appearance of the text in a paragraph. For example, in a left-aligned paragraph (the most common alignment), the text is aligned on the left margin. In a justified paragraph, the text is aligned on both margins.

align text left; centre text; align text right; align text right.
right; justify the text; redraw the text

V II.5.4. JUSTIFYING A TEXT AND MAKING CHANGES

When you justify text, spaces are inserted between words so that the two ends of each line are aligned on both margins. The last line of the paragraph is aligned to the left.

1. Click anywhere in the paragraph to be justified.
2. On the Home **tab**, in **the** Paragraph group, **click**
Justify the text &.

VII.5.5.CREATION OF A SMART LIST WITH A NUMBER

To activate the lines of text in a bulleted or numbered list, select the text and then, under the **home** tab in the **paragraph** group, click on **bullets** or **numbering**. Each line or paragraph becomes a bulleted or numbered list item.

If you start with a blank page ;

1. Place your cursor where you want a bulleted or numbered list.
2. Under the **home** tab, click on the arrow next to **bullets** or **numbering**.
3. Choose a style and start typing.

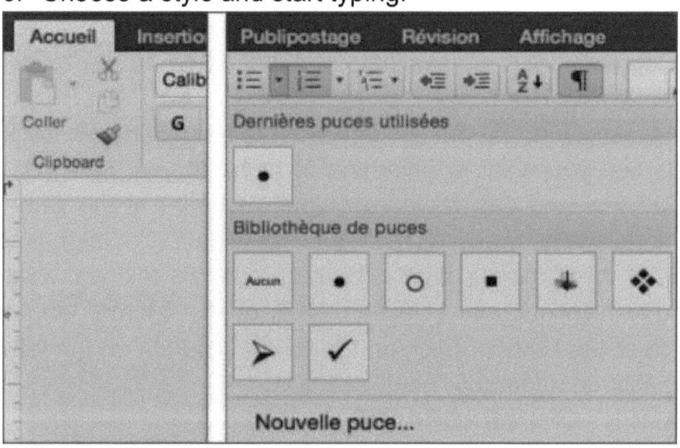

4. Press ENTER each time you want a new chip or number, or press ENTER twice to complete the list.

NB: When you start a paragraph with an asterisk and a space (*), or with the number 1 and a full stop (**1.**), Word displays the **Auto-Correction Options** button and starts to create a bulleted or numbered list. If you don't want to create a bulleted or numbered list, click the **AutoCorrect Options** button, then click **Stop AutoCreate Bulleted Lists** or **Stop AutoCreate Numbered Lists**.

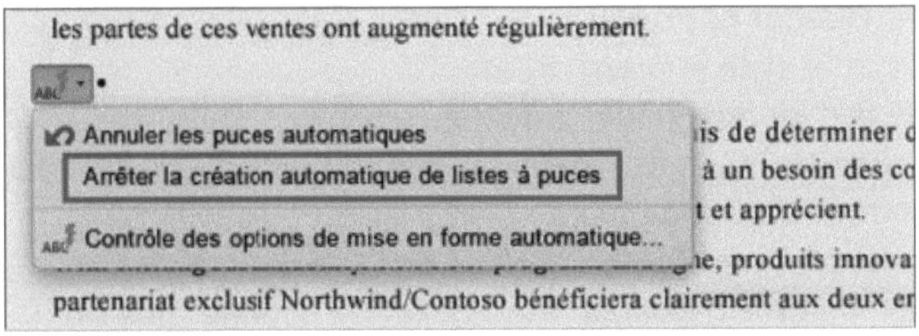

VII.5.6.CREATION OF BORDERS AND GRIDS

You can easily add borders around selected text using Word's Borders feature. Please do the following.

1. Select the texts you are going to add as borders, click on **Home**> **Borders**> **Borders and raster**. See the screenshot:

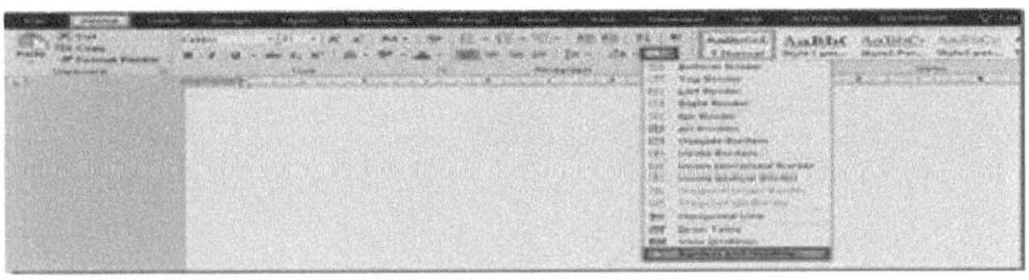

2. in the **Border and Raster** dialog , select the **Top, Bottom, Left** and **Right** border boxes in the **AperQu** section, select **Text** from the **Apply to** drop-down list, then click on **OK** .

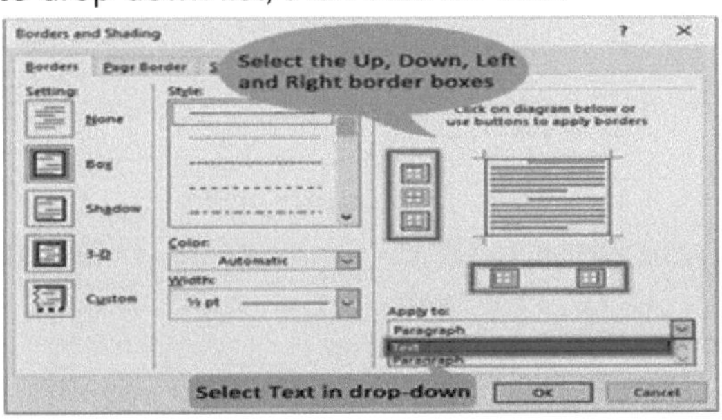

Borders are then added to each line of selected text.

Note: If you simply wish to add a large border around all the selected texts as shown below, please keep the selected **paragraph** in the **Apply to** drop-down list.

VII.5.7.CREATING THE HEADER AND FOOTER

Headers and footers are areas that appear at the top and bottom of each page in a document. They are used to provide additional information and to personalise the document. The elements that can be inserted in these spaces are the page number, the date, a company logo, the title of the document, the name of the file or the name of the author, etc.

1. Go to **Insert> Header** or **Footer**.
2. Choose the header style you wish to use.
3. Add or modify text for the header or footer.
4. To remove a header, such as deleting it from the title page, select it, then tick the **Different first page** box.
5. Select **Close header and footer** or press Esc to exit.

To delete, select **Insert> Header** (or **Footer**) > **Delete header** (or **Delete footer**).

VII.5.8.MODIFYING TEXT MARGINS

Modify the margins of your document to change the layout, then check that all the elements are correctly positioned.

Apply a predefined margin parameter

1. Select **Layout> Margins**.

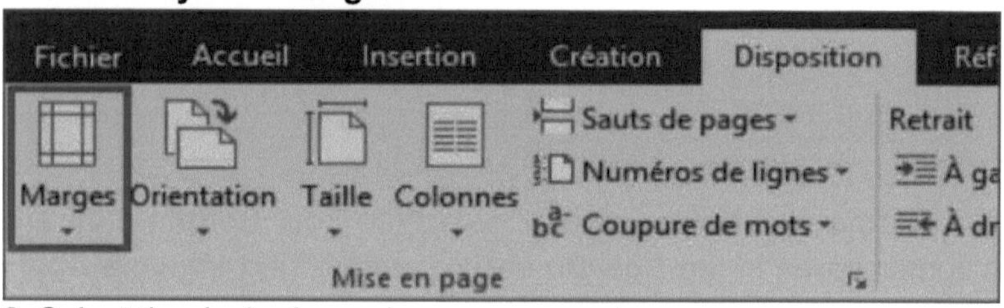

2. Select the desired margin measurements.

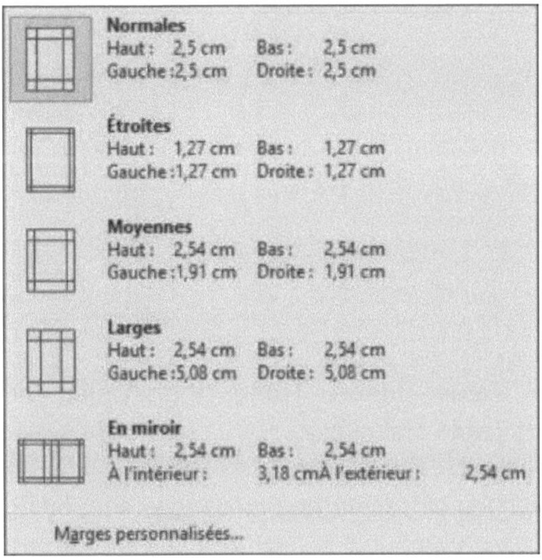

Note: If your document contains several sections, the new margins apply only to the selected sections.

VII.5.9.CHANGING THE ORIENTATION OF THE PAGE

1. To change the orientation of the entire document, select **Layout> Orientation**.
2. Choose **Portrait** or **Landscape**.

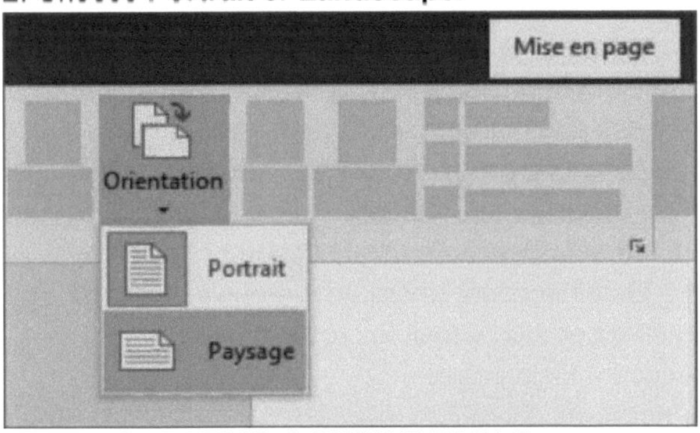

VII.5.10.CREATING A SIMPLE TABLE

Here's how to create an initially symmetrical array.

1. Click in the document where you want to create a table.

First method:

On the **Insert** ribbon, click **Table** then drag the mouse pointer to select the required number of rows and columns.

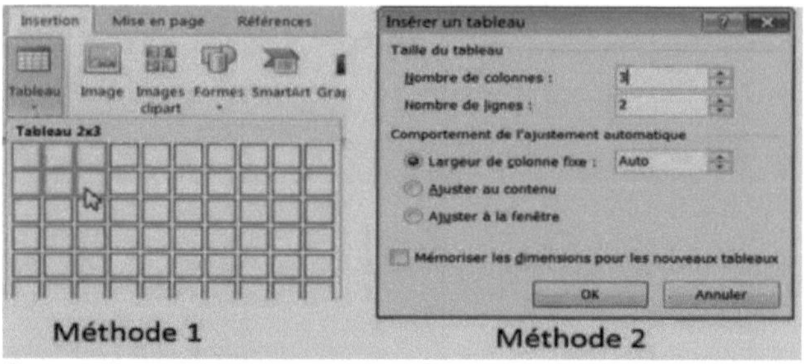

Second method:

On the **Insert** ribbon, click **Table**, **Insert Table**, then enter the appropriate values in **the Insert Table** dialog box.

VII.6.E-MAIL

Electronic *mail* refers to the service of transferring messages sent by an electronic messaging system *via* a computer network (now the Internet) to the electronic mailbox of a recipient chosen by the sender. "Correspondence service enabling electronic messages to be exchanged via a computer network ( ).[8]

VII.6.1.CREATING AN E-MAIL ACCOUNT

First, choose a Google Account type.

This account will be for me or for running a business

NB: When you create a Google Account for your business, you can activate personalisation for businesses. A Business Account also makes it easier to configure the Google business listing, which helps to improve the visibility of your business and manage your information online.

When you create a Google Account, you'll be asked for personal information. By providing accurate information, you're helping to secure your account and make our services more useful to you.

Also if you don't need a Gmail account to create a Google Account. You can use an email address other than Gmail to create one.

1. Go to the Google Account login page.
2. Click on **Create an account**.
3. Enter your name.
4. In the "User name" field, enter a user name.
5. Enter your password and confirm.

NB: When you enter your password on your mobile, the first letter is not case-sensitive.

6. Click **Next**.

[8] https://www.techno-science.net, consulted on 06/10/2023 at 07:04'.

- Optional: Add a telephone number to your account, then confirm.
7. Click **Next**.

Use an existing e-mail address

1. Go to the Google Account login page.
2. Click on **Create an account**.
3. Enter your name.
4. Click on **Use my current e-mail address instead**.
5. Enter your current e-mail address.
6. Click **Next**.
7. Validate your e-mail address using the code sent to your existing e-mail address.
8. Click on **Validate**.

VII.6.2.ACCESS TO AN E-MAIL ACCOUNT

VII.6.2.1.WITH COMPUTER

1. Open Gmail on your computer.
2. Enter the e-mail address corresponding to your Google Account or your telephone number, then your password.

- If the information is already filled in and you need to connect to another account, click on **Use another account**.
- If you find yourself on a page describing Gmail rather than the login page, click **Login** at the top right of the page.

NB: If you connect to a public computer, remember to disconnect before leaving the computer.

VII.6.2.2.WITH ANDROID

On your Android phone or tablet, you can add Gmail accounts, as well as other accounts, in the Gmail application.

1. On your Android phone or tablet, open Gmail .^
2. In the top right-hand corner, tap on your profile photo.
3. Press **Add another account**.
4. Choose the type of account to add.
5. To add your account, follow the on-screen instructions.

VII.6.3.LOGGING OUT OF AN E-MAIL ACCOUNT

VII.6.3.1.LOGGING OFF A COMPUTER

1. Open Gmail.
2. In the top right-hand corner, click on your photo.
3. Click on **Logout**.

VII.6.3.2.DISCONNECTING ON ANOTHER DEVICE

If you've forgotten to log out of your mailbox on another computer, you can log out of Gmail remotely.

1. Open Gmail.
2. In the top right-hand corner, click on your photo.
3. Click on **Manage your Google Account**.
4. Click on **Security**.
5. Under "Your devices", click on **Manage all devices**.
6. Select a device.
7. Click on **Logout**.

VII.7.E-MAIL

Electronic mail, **e-mail** or **email/e-mail**, is a service for transmitting messages sent electronically via a computer network (mainly the Internet) to the mailbox of a recipient chosen by the sender .[9]

VII.7.1.FORWARDING OR FORWARDING AN E-MAIL

1. open the mail you wish to transfer.
2. click on the arrow on the "Replybutton. ...
3. enter the e-mail addresses of your recipients in fields A, Cc and/or Cci. ...
4. click on "Send".

V II.7.2.SENDING A MESSAGE TO SEVERAL RECIPIENTS AT THE SAME TIME

To send the same message to several recipients, enter the different email addresses in the "To" field, separating them with a semicolon.

V II.7.3 USE OF THE C.C AND CCI HEADINGS WHEN SENDING MESSAGES (THEIR ROLE)

The main role of CCI and CC emails is **confidentiality**. While all recipients will be able to see the addresses of other recipients in a Cc e-mail, the addresses in the Bcc field will not be visible to the main recipients.

V II.7.4.SENDING A MESSAGE WITH AN ATTACHED DOCUMENT (WORD, EXCEL, ETC)

1. **Click on File(or office button)> Share(or send),** then choose one of the following options:

Note: The options available vary depending on the Office program you are using.

▪ **Upload to OneDrive** Upload your file to your OneDrive account or you can share it via a direct link or email.

▪ **Attach a copy instead** Choose to attach a file to an e-mail or to attach a PDF file.

2. Enter the recipient aliases, modify the subject and body of the

[9] https://www.techno-science.net, consulted on 30/01/2024 at 12h24'.

message if necessary, then click **Send**.

VII.7.5 DOWNLOADING AN ATTACHED DOCUMENT (Conditions to be observed when downloading an attached document)

To download an attached document simply :

1. Select the Attachments icon in the right-hand panel;
2. Move the mouse over the name of the attachment, select the More icon, then **Download** the file. You can **download** the most recent version in its original format.

VII.7.6.OTHER BUSINESS RELATED SERVICES (e-Banking, e-commerce)

VII.7.6.1. E-BANKING

Electronic banking is **the** term used to describe a **bank that** is available online rather than in person. The user y performs series of actions without having to go anywhere, via a computer or smartphone. They can transfer funds electronically, pay bills and carry out any other action (such as depositing wages automatically).

The **electronic banking service** operates on a computer system that records the ownership of funds and accounts for transfers made. To access the service, the user generally needs to identify himself with an access code (such as a personal identification number).

Online banking is gradually replacing traditional bank services, **interactions faster and smoother**. There are many advantages:

- You can access your bank accounts whenever you want, wherever you want. On holiday, in the underground, on a bank holiday or on a Sunday... access is free and unlimited;
- Online banking keeps you up to date with transactions on your bank account. You receive alerts and notifications in real time. You can often personalise these alerts to suit your preferences;
- Transaction costs are reduced;
- There are a large number of functions, allowing you to carry out many different transactions.

VII.7.6.2. E-COMMERCE

To define the term e-commerce, we can say that it represents the various commercial transactions that take place remotely on the Internet. It is also known as electronic commerce.

Buying on the internet is done through digital objects, often through structures such as websites or social media platforms. Transactions can be carried out in several ways, depending on the form of e-commerce: for private individuals (B2C) or for other companies (B2B).

Purchases can be made via a variety of channels and media: computers, smartphones, tablets, consoles and TV. M-commerce (mobile commerce) is becoming increasingly important: it represents purchases made from platforms selling products or services accessible on smartphones and tablets, a historic change in e-commerce.

THE ADVANTAGES OF E-COMMERCE

1. Reducing overheads

Running an e-commerce site is much more profitable than running a physical shop. You don't need to rent commercial property, just pay for reasonable web hosting. You don't need invest in the security of your commercial property or worry about managing logistics or employees. For an e-commerce site, the typical costs will be the domain name, web hosting, the cost of developing your website, and your inventory. That said, most e-commerce websites also spend money on marketing.

2. No need a physical shop window

Running a physical shop is very complicated. E-commerce will save you a lot of hassle on a day-to-day basis. Renting commercial premises can be expensive, especially if you're in a big city. You also have to pay for electricity, water and Internet access for your commercial space. Security is also a consideration: if you want your physical shop window to be secure, you'll need to invest in cameras and other surveillance equipment. With an e-commerce shop, you can simply set up a website and start selling your products online without having to spend a lot of money on a physical shop.

3. Ability to reach a wider audience

Perhaps the greatest advantage of e-commerce is that it allows you reach a very large audience. A physical shop can only accommodate a certain number of visitors per day, especially if you live in a small town or rural area. With an e-commerce shop, you can reach potential customers all over the world to show them your products. Even if you don't sell your products abroad, you can still reach buyers all over France to boost your sales. This wide reach has even enabled some small e-commerce shops to become iconic brands over time.

4. Scalability and adaptability

Of all the advantages and disadvantages of e-commerce for a business, scalability is one of the most tangible for long-term growth. With a physical shop, your growth will inevitably force you to find a larger retail space at some point. You'll also have to move your stock and equipment, which only complicates things. With e-commerce, your website and shop can grow along with your business, so you won't have to spend a fortune moving to a new, larger retail space.

5. Logistics follow-up

Tracking logistics is an essential part of e-commerce and retail marketing, and it's much easier with a website than with a physical shop. You can outsource your fulfilment logistics to pass on benefits such as 2-day shipping and efficient returns handling to your customers. Everything is recorded electronically, making it easy to track sales and identify trends that will help you develop your business over the long term.

THE DISADVANTAGES OF E-COMMERCE

E-commerce has both advantages and disadvantages for a business, so it's important to be aware of the potential drawbacks too. Running an e-commerce website can be particularly difficult for people who are not very comfortable with computers and technology. Here's what you need to know about the potential drawbacks of e-commerce.

1. Potential security threats

When you sell online, there is always a risk of security threats. A poorly secured website can allow unauthorised users to access your website and view your sensitive data. In rare cases, problems with payment processors can lead to data breaches that put customers' banking information at risk. A large part of setting up an e-commerce site involves securing the website, so business owners often prefer to recruit a professional.

2. Competition

There's a lot of competition in the world of e-commerce, because creating an online shop is as easy as 1-2-3. This is one of the biggest disadvantages of e-commerce, as it means you have to work very hard to promote your shop and drive traffic to your website. Some niches are also very crowded, so you may find it difficult to sell your product in your particular sector. Ultimately, the success of your site will depend on how hard you work to strengthen your online presence.

3. Computer problems

No technical problem can prevent a physical shop from accepting cash, whereas computer problems can be a real hassle for an e-commerce site. If your website suddenly crashes or you have a problem with your payment processor, that downtime can cost you money... and customers. Worse still, resolving these IT problems can cost you even more. Choosing simplicity can help you avoid some of the potential IT problems encountered in e-commerce, but be aware that technological problems can occur.

4. Shipping logistics

Running a physical shop window is easy, just sell the products to customers when they come to shop with you. If you want to sell products over the phone or via a catalogue, you can use a simple shipping service to send a few parcels a week. But for an e-commerce site, you need to understand all the shipping logistics, because every purchase will need to be shipped. Finding the right solution for your shipping and logistics isn't easy, and you don't want to find yourself in the red because of high shipping costs.

5. Limited customer interaction

On an e-commerce site, you 't get interact on a personal level with customers. Some people may prefer that, but the fact is that you can't offer the same personal touch if you're selling online.

CHAPTER VIII

RETENTION OF DATA ON MEDIA

V III.1.DEFINITION

Data storage is the set of methods and technologies used to store digital data. Several types of media are used for data storage, including floppy disks, flash media and hard disks .[10]

V III.2.FLASH DISK (USB KEY)

Flash memory was invented in 1984 by **FUJIO MASUOKA**, a Japanese engineer working for Toshiba. It was first marketed in 1988 as a memory card for digital cameras. Since then, flash memory has evolved rapidly and become an essential element of modern technology.

There are different types of flash memory, including NOR memory and NAND memory. NOR memory is faster but more expensive, while NAND memory is slower but cheaper. NAND memory is most commonly used in consumer electronic devices because of its value for money.

The benefits of flash disk

About the size of a pack of chewing gum, USB flash drives are much smaller than external hard drives. What's more, they don't contain any fragile parts, making them a much more solid and easy-to-carry accessory.

The disadvantages of Flash disk

The risks are numerous, as a simple USB flash drive can infect your computer with all kinds of viruses and malware. In fact, a USB flash drive can pose all kinds of threats to you, your information system and your personal data, and this can cause major damage.

V III.3. CD (CD-R, CD-RW)

A CD (Compact Disk) is a digital optical disc that has been developed to store and play audio recordings. It is a flat, round disc made of

[10] https://ryax.tech/fr, consulted on 30/01/2024 at 13h14'

polycarbonate plastic, usually measuring 12 cm (4.7 in) in diameter. Disc production revolutionised the music industry, replacing analogue formats such as vinyl records and cassettes.

CD operation

A CD uses a laser to read the digital data encoded on its surface. The data is stored as a series of tiny pits and lands, which binary information. When the laser in the CD player shines on the surface of the disc, it reflects differently depending on whether it is in a pit or on land. This reflected light is then converted into electrical signals that can be interpreted as audio or other types of data.

Benefits

- Thematic search and keyword search ;
- Search the full text using a word or expression ;
- Access by several students to the same CD or DVD if it is installed on a network;
- Articles often include **multimedia elements:**

. **Hypertext navigation**: the links take you further on the subject, to an illustration, etc.

. **Images** (maps, diagrams, photographs, drawings, etc.): can be saved, enlarged, imported into a job or printed.

- **Sounds** you can listen to again and again.
- **Video sequences** that can be recorded and incorporated into a presentation.
- Copy extracts to be quoted in full or reworded for note-taking;
- You can save, export and print all or part of a text with certain CD-DVDs.

Disadvantages

- Not always up to date, although this medium is less expensive than print to update;
- Not all CD-DVDs provide access to information in the same way. So you need to familiarise yourself with each one;
- If the CD or DVD is not on the network, you need to borrow it and reserve a computer with a CD or DVD drive.

VIII.4.EXTERNAL HARD DISK(BOX)

An external hard drive is extra storage space that lets you **keep your files,** back them up and keep them safe .[11]

To make sure you don't lose any of your data or multimedia files on your laptop or desktop computer, remember to back them up regularly on an external hard drive.

How an external hard drive works

The **external hard drive** is installed in a hard drive enclosure connected to your computer. It is made up of several ceramic or metal discs, operating one on top of the other.

Electromagnets, or read/write heads, transmit or receive data by moving sideways. Using a converter, they transform the computer's language into a positive or negative magnetic field that polarises the surface of the disc over a defined area. The heads are thus raised and lowered at a precise point on the disc in an ultra-fast rotating movement.

When reading or writing is complete, the heads move into a safe position to prevent damage and protect the stored data.

There are now fully electronic external SSD disks which, although faster, are not yet capable of storing large quantities of data.

THE STORAGE CAPACITY OF AN EXTERNAL HARD DRIVE

The storage capacity must be adapted to your needs. If you are only using this external hard drive to store your files before a business trip, and it is not intended as a backup for all your data, then a 1 TB external hard drive may be sufficient. If, on the other hand, you want to store all your data as a complete backup, then you need to consider the **capacity of the external hard drive** you need.

To find out this capacity, go to the file manager, right-click and then click on "properties". This will give you the total capacity of your hard drive and the space occupied by your data.

We recommend that you **buy an external hard drive** with at least the same capacity as your current equipment, if not more, to anticipate your needs and avoid having to reinvest in a higher-capacity model later on.

EXTERNAL HARD DRIVE CONNECTORS

Most external hard drives are connected to your computer via USB 3.0 or 3.1. Some professional models may have a SATA connection. So be sure to check whether your PC has this external connection.

CHOOSING AN HDD OR SSD EXTERNAL HARD DRIVE

Most external hard drives are mechanical and are also known as HDDs.

---

[11] https://www.inmac-wstore.com, consulted on 30/01/2024 at 14h16'

These models offer a large amount of storage capacity (from 4TB to 8TB for the most powerful models). They are affordable and the most popular for home use.

An external SSD has no internal mechanics but flash memory, which is still limited. The advantage of this external SSD drive is its speed of execution, shorter latency time and faster transfer rate. On the other hand, this SSD external hard drive won't be useful if you want to back up your entire hard drive. Its price is higher than an HHD because of the high cost of manufacturing flash memory.

BIBLIOGRAPHY

❖ **Books:**

- Curriculum National des Humanites Techniques Commercials, March 2014;
- Jacques LONCHAMP, introduction aux systemes informatique, Paris, Dunod, 2011.

❖ **Websites:**

- https://www.excel-pratique.com
- https://intia.fr
- https://www.fiche-paie.net
- https://www.morpheus-formation.fr
- https://www.sage.com
- https://www.techno-science.net
- https://www.inmac-wstore.com
- https://barrazacarlos.com
- https://www.larousse.fr

MIX
Papier aus verantwortungsvollen Quellen
Paper from responsible sources
FSC® C105338

Printed by Books on Demand GmbH, Norderstedt / Germany